# BLUEBIRDS!

By
Steve Grooms
and
Dick Peterson

NORTHWORD
PRESS, INC
P.O. Box 1360
Minocqua, WI 54548

**Library of Congress Cataloging-in-Publication Data**

Grooms, Steve.
Bluebirds / by Steve Grooms and Dick Peterson.
p. cm. -- (Camp & cottage collection : 2. Wildlife)
Includes bibliographical references.
ISBN 1-55971-095-0 : $ 16.95
1. Bluebirds. 2. Bluebirds--Pictorial works. I. Peterson, Dick. II. Title. III. Series : Camp & cottage collection ; 2. IV. Series : Camp & cottage collection. Wildlife.
QL696.P288G76 1991
598.8'42--dc20 91-9379
CIP


Box 1360, Minocqua, WI 54548



Designed by Mary A. Shafer
Typeset by Cavanaugh Ink.
Cover Photograph by Steve Maslowski
ISBN 1-55971-095-0

Printed and bound in Singapore.

# Contents

# Author Biographies

**Steve Grooms** has a long history of writing for the outdoors. Following his receipt of a Bachelor's degree in American Studies from Grinnell College in Iowa, he went on to earn his Master of Arts in the same field from the University of Minnesota. After finishing his studies, he secured a position as editor of *Fins & Feathers*, a magazine dealing with the outdoors and sporting life. There he remained for eight years, prior to striking out on his own as a freelance writer in 1980.

His freelance subjects range from scientific pieces for outdoors publications to scenic pieces for *Wisconsin Trails* magazine. He is also a field editor for *Pheasants Forever*, a pheasant conservation organization and publication, as well as holding a similar position with *Trout* magazine, also a conservation-oriented publication.

Steve lives with his wife Kathe and their daughter, Molly, in St. Paul, Minnesota. They travel frequently to their recreational property on the shores of Lake Superior near Cornucopia, Wisconsin, where they indulge in their shared love of the outdoors.

With **Bluebirds**, Steve hopes to broaden his range of outdoor subjects to include natural history matter.

**Dick Peterson**, affectionately known by hundreds of fellow bluebird enthusiasts as "Mr. Bluebird," is best known for his research on bluebird nesting box design. He built and tested over 4,000 different box designs over twelve years, finally arriving at the now-familiar variation that bears his name. Most bluebird enthusiasts consider this to be absolutely the best nesting box design in use today.

Dick and his wife Vi, who currently reside in Brooklyn Center, Minnesota, for many years maintained a nesting box trail consisting of 472 units, which they would check ever week or so.

Very active in developing and presenting bluebird programs to 4-H clubs and Boy Scout troops, the Petersons helped start the Bluebird Recovery Program of Minnesota, one of the most successful such programs in the country.

***Editor's Note:***

***Bluebirds!*** *was an interesting partnership between Steve Grooms and Dick Peterson. While they share co-authorship, it should be noted that Steve provided the sentences and Dick the ideas and inspiration. Together they gave a voice to the bluebirds' story.*

*All the material in the sidebars not specifically credited to others was provided by Dick Peterson – the result of a lifetime thinking about and talking about his favorite subject.*

# Preface

*Photo Page 3: This young bluebird still wears some of the spotty marks of juvenile thrushes.*

*– Bill Marchel Photo*

This book tells one of the most remarkable stories in the history of relations between humans and animals. It is, in every sense, a love story.

Americans long have identified bluebirds with all that is beautiful and appealing in the animal world. And why not? Bluebirds are among the loveliest of birds. It is the bird, as Henry Thoreau so poetically noted, that "carries the sky on his back." Gentle and friendly, bluebirds regard humans with amiable trust. Among the earliest northward migrators, bluebirds inevitably have come to be seen as symbols of hope.

Few birds have appeared more frequently in songs and poems. When Judy Garland sang of her yearning for a happy land somewhere over the rainbow, the bird she imagined flying there was a bluebird. Another popular song exhorts us to: "Remember this, life is no abyss. Somewhere there's a bluebird of happiness." The lyricist had it right. With due respect to other delightful birds, the "Baltimore Oriole of happiness" simply doesn't sound right.

But the bird that best symbolizes happiness has not had a happy history in the twentieth century.These little thrushes, once common even in our cities, have become so rare that most contemporary Americans have not seen one.

The decline in bluebird numbers is a direct result of human activities. Unthinkingly, men have destroyed much bluebird habitat. Humans also introduced two alien species: the house sparrow and the starling, which have plagued bluebirds ever since, killing incalculable numbers of bluebirds each year and preventing many of the survivors from reproducing. Ugly, tuneless and nasty in their habits, sparrows and starlings are the antithesis of bluebirds.

But this, remember, is a love story. When bluebird populations plummeted and it even seemed possible that they might disappear forever, some people who loved them began to act. Their efforts have won a far more promising future for bluebirds.

Today, thousands of people are actively involved in the effort to bring bluebirds back to abundance. They hike their bluebird trails, checking and tending the nest boxes. They build boxes which they give away to strangers. They fight unending battles with sparrows, snakes and raccoons. They give presentations to youth groups, explaining the problems of bluebirds and teaching youngsters to build nest boxes. Above all, they make it possible for bluebirds to make the world a more joyful place by filling it up with baby bluebirds.

Perhaps you would like to join them.

If you become concerned about the fate of some animal, there is usually little you can do. You can join conservation groups and make donations. But you probably cannot personally go into the elephant conservation business, for example, by raising elephants in your yard. You cannot hold timber wolf pups in your hands, pups that you helped to enter the world.

In this respect, the fans of bluebirds enjoy a wonderful advantage. Anyone living in the range of the eastern bluebird can work for bluebirds and *with* bluebirds. While you are helping bluebird populations in general, you also will be helping some bluebirds in particular. The birds that set up housekeeping in your nest boxes will get to know you personally. They will be glad to see you. One day you will see eggs in one of your boxes. In a short time those eggs will become baby bluebirds, and, yes, you can touch them. At that point, they will be far more than just *symbols* of happiness to you.

Helping bluebirds is a deeply satisfying hobby and a unique adventure in conservation. The authors of this book invite you to experience for yourself the joys of enriching this world by filling it with bluebirds.

*Photo Page 4: Young bluebirds like this often help feed even younger birds.*

*– Ted Thousand Photo*

*Photo Page 6: The eastern bluebird, having fallen to dangerously low population levels, is recovering now.*

*– Ted Thousand Photo*

# A Love Affair With Bluebirds

On a sunny afternoon in late May, a woman kneels in a pasture to observe the bluebird nest box she calls N-18. It is a glorious day, fragrant with blooming life. Butterflies float lazily over dandelions strewn across the pasture like the stars of the Milky Way.

She doesn't notice. Her binoculars and attention are focussed on the activity at N-18.

Two bluebirds, a male and his mate, bob in the branches of an apple tree in an abandoned orchard. They face the nest box and call to their young. Though the music of bluebirds is usually sweet and flutelike the call they make today is oddly intense. They *want* something.

The boldest of the four babies perches hesitantly with his head just outside the hole.The cedar walls of the dim nest box are all he has known of the world for the nearly three weeks he has been in it. Now he peers out at the riot of colors and shapes that makes up the outside world. His father glides toward the hole with a plump, mint-green caterpillar in his mouth. Fluttering inches in front of the hesitant baby, the male teases him with the morsel, then returns to the apple tree. Food will not come to the youngster. For the first time in his life, he must go to it.

The baby rocks a bit, caught in classic approach-avoidance tension. He's going to go! No, he isn't. He's going to go! Nope, not yet. He's . . .

He's gone!

The baby tips forward into the sunlight and hits the air with madly buzzing wings. He zooms to a low branch of the apple tree. In one of nature's routine miracles, the baby bluebird manages flight the first time he attempts it. His first flying lesson is also his first solo.

The kneeling woman smiles with the beatific pride of a Renaissance madonna as she watches the fledglings coming out of the nest box. Though she has helped many bluebird pairs nest and rear their young, before today she has never witnessed the drama of a first flight. She has a unique relationship with these birds. They know her on sight. They know the sound of her voice. Though they

*Spread pages 10-11: Sharp storms can virtually wipe out bluebird populations in a given area.*

*– Steve Kirkpatrick Photo*

*Opposite: Bluebirds can survive cold weather if they have access to food.*

*– Steve Kirkpatrick Photo*

***The bluebird, instantly winsome to young and old and to people of modern or traditional sensibilities alike, is American idealism personified . . . a flying piece of sky, a living poem, a crystal note, an emblem of nature's moral conscience.***

*– Stanwyn G. Shetler*

***The first flight of the babies is truly amazing. Here these little guys have never flown before in their lives, yet they do it right the first time. I once watched this one family of fledglings come out of the box. They flew 120 feet to the top of an aspen tree and all landed within three feet of each other. So they weren't flying, they were flying under control, the very first time!***

Opposite:
– Dick Peterson Photo

trust her, they cannot know she has done everything in her power to ease life's difficulties for them. Once she even dealt death to enemies–a pair of house sparrows–that threatened to kill "her" bluebirds. She has been these birds' benefactor, their fairy godmother, their guardian angel. She is one of thousands of bluebird guardians.

Articles about the eastern bluebird usually say something like, "Its sweet song and appealing behavior make the bluebird one of America's most liked birds." True enough, but such pallid phrases fail to catch the singular and marvelous relationship between bluebirds and the humans who aid them. *No* bird in America is more lovable or more passionately loved. Not even loons.

There are many reasons humans find bluebirds appealing. To begin with, they are beautiful. Inexperienced birders might see another bird, an indigo bunting perhaps, and think it is a bluebird. But when you see a male bluebird, there can be no doubt. No other bird in America is so wonderfully, so intensely blue. While most songbirds are either beautiful *or* lovely to hear, the bluebird is both. Ornithologist Thomas S. Roberts called the mellow warble of the bluebird "one of the sweetest, most confiding and loving sounds in nature."

People see bluebirds as symbols of hope. Their northward migration brings music and beauty to land that has slumbered through the numbing whiteness of winter and the chill and mud of early spring. Bluebirds are early migrators, sometimes paying a terrible price for their eagerness when winter delivers a final stiff kick. But when they come, bluebirds redeem nature's promise that the

***Got a bluebird***
***on my shoulder!***
***It's the truth,***
***It's factual!***
***Everything is***
***satisfactual!***

*– from "The Song of the South"*

***When I go out in my backyard, the bluebirds all come out to see me and show off. They chirp to me and I chirp to them. If I'm going to feed them, I whistle and they all gather on the picnic table where I put the food.***

*– Delores Wendt*

*Preceding Spread: Once a familiar bird, the eastern bluebird has become so rare that few adults today have seen one.*

*– Dick Peterson Photo*

*Opposite: The bluebird has been widely celebrated in songs and literature, often associated with beauty, family values and hope.*

*– Steve Maslowski Photo*

near-death of winter will be followed by a renewal of life. Beyond that, bluebirds are simply *likable*. They eat undesirable insects without doing any harm to humans. The courtship of bluebirds, gentle and rapturous, is one of the most endearing spectacles in nature. Adult bluebirds raise their young with devotion and tender concern. Both parents share in this care, for bluebirds seem to want to do everything in pairs or as families.

No matter how often scientists tell us not to, people relate to animals anthropomorphically. In these terms, bluebirds are enormously appealing. In song, personal appearance and social habits, bluebirds epitomize desirable human traits. If bluebirds were people, they would be respected citizens who raise their families with exemplary devotion, lead productive lives and contribute generously to charities. And they would surely be featured soloists in church choirs on Sunday mornings!

***My wife and I were coming back from Gettysburg, Pennsylvania, from a national bluebird conservation meeting. We crossed from Canada at a U.S. Customs station in Michigan. The officer wanted to know where we'd been and what we'd been doing. When we said we'd been meeting about bluebirds, he got excited. He'd been trying to get bluebirds with no luck. Cars were starting to back up behind us. We said we did real well. So he wanted to see our boxes. We showed him. Now there were REALLY a lot of cars behind ours. We worried about that, but he said, "Oh heck, let 'em wait! This is more important!" Then he wanted a brochure we had on bluebird recovery. We couldn't find it, so pretty soon all three of us were tearing the car apart, looking for that brochure. We had to laugh about that later, wondering how it looked to all those cars behind us. They probably couldn't figure why a Customs agent was tearing down the car of those two sweet-looking middle-aged folks! That's what happens when you get bluebird people together!***

*– Richard Hjort*

*Opposite: A banded juvenile.*

*– Dick Peterson Photo*

***If the warble of the first bluebird does not thrill you, know that the morning and spring of your life are past.***

*– Henry D. Thoreau*

There is more. Few birds are as trusting or quick to accept the friendship of humans. Bluebirds form friendly bonds with the people who feed them or check their nests. Adult bluebirds go out of their way to "greet" familiar trail monitors, flying out and calling to them, following them as they leave. If you hold your hand by the hole of a nesting box you check regularly, the adults will probably perch on your finger to feed their young.

Who could not love such a bird?

What else but love could motivate a gentle person who adores birds to trap and kill (often by hand) vast numbers of house sparrows each year? Killing birds is simply not a natural act for people who identify themselves as "bird-lovers." Yet it is not unusual for a bluebirder to kill a thousand sparrows a year, explaining, "You lose your inhibitions quickly when you see what sparrows do to your bluebirds!"

Love for bluebirds inspired Dave Ahlgren of Stillwater, Minnesota, to build bluebird nest boxes which he sells at cost to anyone interested in putting them up. Dave is an airline pilot with a busy schedule, so he makes boxes in his "spare" time. Many other people build birdhouses or feeders, of course, but few can match Dave Ahlgren's dedication: he has built *over 20,000* bluebird nest boxes.

The same love touched John and Norah Lane, of Brandon, Manitoba. In 1959, Jack founded the Brandon Junior Birders, a group of youngsters who built nest boxes. The group established a trail of bluebird boxes. It was lengthened until it became the longest bluebird trail in the world. Today that trail stretches from North Battleford, Saskatchewan, to MacGregor, Manitoba. With its associated side-trails, this trail now covers 2,500 miles, and produces several thousand young bluebirds annually. When her husband died, Norah, at age 67, learned to drive a car just so she could continue to monitor his trails.

For a surprising number of people, helping bluebirds is their main recreation and their greatest source of joy in life. Such people are apt to admit, perhaps with an embarrassed grin, "I guess you'd say I have a love affair with bluebirds!"

And, there is a final reason people go to such extraordinary lengths to help this species. Bluebirds not only accept the help of humans, they absolutely need it.

## A LOVE AFFAIR WITH BLUEBIRDS

The bluebird population has dropped to frighteningly low levels. Because people are the cause, it is only fitting that people should work to salvage a secure future for this exquisite songbird. Bluebirds aren't the only species that needs or deserves such help, but bluebirds offer unique rewards for the people who help them. Usually, people concerned about a species have to work for it from a distance: writing checks to pay for habitat restoration or lobbying for legislation to undo past ecological mistakes.

It is different with bluebirds. Putting up and tending nest boxes is the best, most rewarding way the average person can help them. Bluebird trailing is the ultimate hands-on, individual, grassroots conservation program. It can be done by virtually anyone who can walk. There is no better way to expose children to the delights of the natural world than to teach them to care for bluebirds. Monitoring a bluebird trail is a rewarding hobby for many older people, including active bluebirders in their 70s, 80s and 90s.

What is ultimately most remarkable about bluebirds is the unique relationship between them and the humans who love them so deeply, who feed, shelter and defend them. Above all, they arrange ideal nesting circumstances so existing bluebirds have the best possible chance to bring more of their delightful kind into the world.

The bluebirds respond by taking good advantage of these efforts and by accepting their helpers with open trust and affection. It is not a one-way relationship.

It's no wonder that so many people have a love affair with bluebirds.

***I don't go along with people who insist that these are just "dumb birds" who are governed by nothing but instinct. They truly do get to know the people who monitor the boxes. I had one family of bluebirds for three years that recognized me and would fly way out to say hello when I came. Each spring when they showed up, they already acted friendly toward me like they knew me from before. Even when I left, they'd fly along with me for a hundred yards or so until I got too close to the nest box.***

*Opposite: A male bluebird preens his feathers.*

*– Steve Maslowski Photo*

# North America's Bluebirds

North America has three species of bluebirds: the eastern, mountain and western bluebird. All belong to the *Turdidae* (TUR-dih-dee) or thrush family. Near relatives of the thrushes include warblers, wrens, dippers and flycatchers.

THRUSHES

Thrushes are among the most widespread of birds. They occur most places in the world except Antarctica and some oceanic islands. Most thrushes are attractive birds with enchanting voices. Popular European thrushes include the nightingale and song thrush. The English robin, which closely resembles the bluebird, is a thrush. Among North America's thrushes are the wood thrush, hermit thrush, Swainson's thrush, veery and the ubiquitous robin.

No family of birds has more accomplished singers. The haunting panpipe notes of the veery add mystery and charm to America's woodlands. The loveliest singer of all might be the hermit thrush, whose delicate flutelike notes have earned it the nickname "swamp angel." Even the familiar robin sings well, carolling the sunset with inventive up-and-down whistles.

Thrushes range from four to thirteen inches in length. They have stout legs and perching feet. All are primarily ground-based insect-eaters. Thrushes have ten primaries in each wing and a distinctive scaled leg pattern called the "booted tarsus."

NORTH AMERICA'S BLUEBIRDS

Bluebirds are indigenous to North America and occur nowhere else. America's early settlers often called bluebirds "blue robins" because they are so much like England's robin. All bluebirds have a "buoyant" up-and-down flight. They often appear hunched when perched. Bluebirds spend much of their time perched near the ground on branches of trees or shrubs, on fences or on utility wires. Their most typical feeding pattern involves fluttering to the ground to seize insects. There is some habitat overlap between the three bluebirds. Colorado is

*Spread Pages 24-25: A juvenile bluebird at sunset.*

*– Dick Peterson Photo*

*Opposite: The mountain bluebird sings well, but confines his singing mostly to early morning moments.*

*– Steve Maslowski Photo*

***But no blue, not even the brightest summer sky, seems as blue as the bluebirds of spring.***

*– Ron Hirschi*

one of the few areas where all three species nest. There are records of several hybrids of eastern bluebirds with both mountain and western bluebirds.

EASTERN BLUEBIRD

The best known of North America's bluebirds is the eastern bluebird, *Sialia sialis* (sigh-AY-lih-ah SIGH-al-iss).

In appearance, the eastern bluebird is a smaller, more delicate and much more colorful version of the robin. Bluebirds are two-thirds the size of a robin, at about seven inches in length. The male eastern bluebird shares the robin's rich red-orange breast and white underbelly. But where the robin is dark gray (on the head, back and tail) the bluebird is azure, the pure blue of an unclouded sky. Bluebird males have a faint black and white barring on the tips of the wing primaries and a small white throat patch and a faint white lower eye ring. The female eastern bluebird is a muted version of the male. The grayish juveniles have speckled breasts and white back spots. They resemble baby robins.

Efforts at rendering the music of bluebirds in words mostly show how limited language can be. Some hear the call as "*Chir-wi! Chir-wi!*" To others, it sounds like "*Tru-ally, Tru-ally!*" The Audubon bird call, a wood barrel with a metal insert, makes twitterings that resemble the winsome chirruping of bluebirds. Bluebird couples do a great deal of singing: to each other, to their young and to the world. Their gentle warblings express an enormous

***Some people just won't believe they can be brought back. When I first began to work for bluebirds, many people had never seen one. They wouldn't believe conservation could work. Now I can invite people to my trails, telling them they'll see more bluebirds than robins! And they do. But when I talk to people in western states about saving the mountain bluebird, I see the same pessimism I used to encounter in the Midwest.***

*Opposite: A mountain bluebird female awaits her opportunity to feed the nestlings.*

*– Alan Carey Photo*

***I've got a friend who has a bluebird trail out by a senior citizens' home, and he often invites them over to walk his trail. He says, "When they see a bluebird, I swear they get ten years younger!" It's just something about bluebirds.***

*Following Spread: One of the bluest birds in nature, a male mountain bluebird.*

*– Steve Maslowski Photo*

*Opposite: A female mountain bluebird. Like the Eastern Bluebird, mountain bluebirds need help.*

*– Steve Maslowski Photo*

***Some people say the mountain bluebird is bigger than the eastern bluebird and needs a bigger entry hole in the box, but I doubt that. I've photographed mountain bluebirds nesting in boxes on a farm in western Minnesota. They were the same size as our regular bluebirds and had no trouble using the standard entry hole.***

range of emotions. Most touching of all is the singing done by the male during courtship.

The range of the eastern bluebird basically comprises the eastern two-thirds of the United States, from the eastern seaboard westward to the feet of the Rocky Mountains. Bluebirds summer as far north as southern Canada, even farther north along the Maritime Provinces.

Eastern bluebirds winter primarily in the middle and southern states. Bluebirds that nest in the far north generally winter south of the 40° latitude line. Some wintering bluebirds venture as far south as Mexico and Nicaragua. Most bluebirds that nest south of the Great Lakes watershed are non-migratory birds.

## MOUNTAIN BLUEBIRD

The mountain bluebird, *Sialia currucoides* (sigh-AY-lih-ah cure-you-COY-deez), is truly a blue bird. His upper parts are the intense blue of the eastern bluebird, to which the mountain bluebird adds a light blue breast and belly. The mountain bluebird is about the same size as the eastern bluebird.

As the name suggests, the mountain bluebird is normally a bird of the high country. Mountain bluebirds summer from the Pacific coast east through and somewhat past the Rockies, and from the Mexican border north to Alaska. They are generally found within an elevation band starting at 5,000 feet and ending just below the timberline,

***The bluebird's disposition is typical of all that is sweet and amiable. His song of love; even his fall call-note – TUR-WEE, TUR-WEE – is soft and gentle. So associated is his voice with the birth and death of the seasons that to me his song is freighted with all the gladness of springtime, while the sad notes of the birds passing southward tell me more plainly than the falling leaves that the year is dying.***

*– Frank M. Chapman*

about 10,000 to 12,000 feet. Mountain bluebirds winter in the Southwest, primarily in Texas, New Mexico and Arizona. In California, most of the mountain bluebirds do not migrate. Mountain bluebirds inhabit meadows, pine ridges and groves of aspens and cottonwoods. They often frequent ranch buildings. Though they eat slightly different species of insects, their feeding habits are identical to those of the eastern bluebird.

The song of the mountain bluebird is somewhat more robin-like than the eastern bluebirds. Alas, mountain bluebirds sing less than eastern bluebirds. While the eastern bluebird sings throughout the day, especially at courting time, mountain and western bluebirds mostly confine singing to early dawn when few humans are up and about to enjoy their music.

The mountain bluebird is the state bird of both Idaho and Nevada.

***Bluebirds seem to have a second lanuage – body language – that they use to make important points. Of course, they're always singing and chattering. But when they have something special to say, like when they're defending territory or courting, the body language really comes into play.***

## WESTERN BLUEBIRD

The western bluebird, *Sialia mexicana* (sigh-AY-lih-ah meks-ih-CANE-ah), has a red breast like the eastern but a blue throat and rusty back. The female and juveniles are browner than the eastern bluebird. Their size, again, is identical to the eastern bluebird's.Western bluebirds are the least abundant of America's bluebirds. They are found west of the Rockies, from the Canadian border to the Mexican border. They inhabit park-like woodlands, scattered conifers and hardwoods in the mountains. In the fall they often gather in flocks. The winter migration takes them to western Texas, New Mexico and southeastern Arizona. Many California, Arizona and New Mexico western bluebirds are permanent, non-migratory residents. Conservationists are especially concerned about the future of this stunning thrush.

***Full of innocent vivacity, warbling its ever pleasing notes, and familiar as any bird can be in its natural freedom, it is one of the most agreeable of our feathered favorites. The pure azure of its mantle, and the glow of its breast, render it conspicuous, as it flits through the orchards and gardens, crosses the fields or meadows, or hops along by the roadside.***

*–John James Audubon*

*Top: Mountain bluebirds feed mostly on insects.*

*– Steve Maslowski Photo*

*Bottom: A male western bluebird with a morsel for his nestlings.*

*– Steve Maslowski Photo*

# The Life of the Eastern Bluebird

*Spread Pages 36-37: Mountain bluebirds use different habitat, but otherwise share the habits of eastern bluebirds.*

*– Steve Maslowski Photo*

*Opposite: Bluebirds learn to relax about the presence of humans who monitor their boxes.*

*– Dick Peterson Photo*

Many of the eastern bluebirds' habits are natural consequences of the way they feed. Bluebirds are not adept at catching bugs on the wing, though they can do it. They mainly practice what is called "hawking," perching until they spot their prey, then flying down to seize it. Occasionally bluebirds hover over an insect, apparently trying to flush it out where they can snatch it. Since bluebirds mainly feed on ground-dwelling insects, they perch close to the ground.

Because bluebirds depend on spotting their prey from a distance, they only feed efficiently in open spaces where the grass is short, sparse or intermittent. Other birds are adapted to feeding on insects in heavy vegetation, but not bluebirds. They are birds of sunny openings where the grass is short or patchy. In grass over knee-height, they lose feeding efficiency.

Ideal bluebird habitat combines some sort of perch overlooking a sunlit clearing. Today, that ideal is probably a farm pasture. Pastures usually have scattered trees and fences, and grass that is cropped short by cattle or horses. Good bluebird habitat can be found around gardens, parks, gravel pits, idle orchards, golf courses, meadows, farms and woodland openings. Country roads with fences and utility lines adjacent to grassy openings also make good habitat.

Bluebirds once were common "backyard" birds that nested in towns, just as their cousin, the robin, does now. When the starling and the house sparrow became common in cities, bluebirds were forced to retreat to rural areas and the outer fringes of suburbs. Bluebirds often thrive where agricultural lands merge with expanding suburbs. Such areas tend to fill with homes built on lots bigger than are found in cities. They are owned by people who moved "to the country" to be near wildlife, so they often put up feeders and nest boxes.

## FOODS

By some estimates, insects constitute 70 percent of the diet of bluebirds across the year. When insects are

abundant in spring and summer, bluebirds eat little else; bugs and caterpillars make up 90 percent of their summer diet. They eat berries and wild fruits when insects, in late summer and fall, are less available. Even the winter diet of bluebirds is 60 percent insects. Among insects eaten by bluebirds are grasshoppers, katydids, crickets, beetles, butterflies, flies, dragonflies, cutworms, maggots, corn borers, alfalfa beetles, spiders, millipedes, centipedes, sow bugs and caterpillars of many species.

Berries and fruits favored by bluebirds include blackberries, pin cherries, chokecherries, bayberries, wild grapes, pokeberries, and the fruit of the honeysuckle, Virginia creeper, red cedar and dogwood. Bluebirds have even been known to eat snails, earthworms, small lizards and tree frogs.

With such a diverse diet, it wouldn't seem likely that bluebirds would ever starve. Yet nestlings frequently die of malnutrition when adverse weather makes insects unavailable for a few days in spring or early summer.

Conservationists also fear wintering bluebirds might now face food shortages severe enough to limit their numbers. Urban development and intensive agriculture have eliminated important food sources. At the same time, the European starling has spread into prime bluebird habitat, even wild areas. Starlings now strip trees and shrubs of the food bluebirds depend upon in winter.

COURTSHIP

A "secondary cavity-nester," the bluebird lacks the special head and beak adaptations that enable woodpeckers and flickers to hammer openings out of soft wood.Since bluebirds cannot create their own cavities, they must use those made by other birds. Bluebirds mostly nest in cavities made by downy, hairy, red-headed, red-bellied and (less frequently) pileated woodpeckers.

Bluebirds migrate very early in spring. They probably have to. Their strategy for claiming the limited number of cavities is to be first in line. That strategy carries risks. Unusually harsh weather in early spring will occasionally kill large numbers of bluebirds. Bluebirds migrate into northern states in the first weeks of March, arriving in Canada in the early weeks of April. They typically show

*Opposite: Bluebird nestlings, three days old.*

*– Dick Peterson Photo*

***I've seen horsehair in a bluebird nest only once, built by a bird nesting right by a stable. The whole nest was woven from horsehairs. It was really done beautifully.***

***When bluebird males are fighting over territory, it is really something! They get each other down on the ground, rolling and kicking up a dust cloud in a head-over-heels brawl. They are serious!***

1019

up very shortly after the snowcap disappears. They come when the fields are drab and rivers are swollen with snowmelt water.

Bluebird courtship is not as rigidly patterned as it is with many birds. The male initiates courtship activities. After finding one or more potential nesting sites, he entices his mate to accept one. Copulation between mated birds usually begins even before nest building, though it may continue after the female begins building the nest.

The courtship between the mated pair is beautiful to see or hear. The male warbles seductively to his mate. He engages in a series of impressive displays, including poses with a widespread tail and extended wings. He perches beside her, caressing and singing to her. He brings her choice food items. Popping in and out of the nesting cavity, he endeavors to persuade her to inspect it. She, at first, feigns indifference. But his suit is irresistible, delivered with singing that has been described as "all but unbearable ecstasy." The pair bond is strong between mating bluebirds, though either the female or male might mate with two partners in a season. Courtship concludes when the female signals her acceptance of a nesting cavity by entering it. The pair at this time goes through a variety of displays, accompanied by rhapsodic singing and tails that vibrate in a blur of bliss.

Bluebirds defend their territory against other bluebirds, though not against other species. Both sexes engage in aggressive territorial displays, but only against their own sex; females bluebirds drive off other female bluebirds,

***I was in a blind once, photographing bluebirds, when one came along with a huge grasshopper in his mouth. He was holding it gently. The grasshopper stuck his foot against the bluebird's face and kicked free. Was that bluebird mad! He hovered over the grass just like a kestrel before snatching that grasshopper again. Then he went to a hard gravel road and pounded the grasshopper on it so he'd never do that again!***

*Opposite: Bluebirds typically land at a hole with one foot on the edge and one grasping down below.*

*– Dick Peterson Photo*

***I was visiting some friends once who had two ponds in a sheep yard. This day, mayflies were hatching from the ponds. A pair of bluebirds were feeding some young, about 12 days old. Every time a mayfly would rise about 20 feet above the pond, the bluebirds would have it. They made it look so easy.***

while males drive off males. Bluebirds try to keep others bluebirds at least 100 yards away in the nesting season. They later mix comfortably in larger groups during migration and through winter.

NESTING

Once she accepts a cavity, the female bluebird takes charge and, in fact, often becomes quite bossy. After selecting a nesting site the female begins building a nest. This could be hours or days later. The male often hauls in materials, but the female constructs the nest alone.

Bluebird nests are simple, clean and neat. A typical bluebird nest is constructed with dry grass and lined with softer materials, such as finer grasses, horsehairs or (rarely) feathers. Thin grass, pine needles, weed stems or even fine twigs are sometimes used in the lower nest. Compared to other birds, the nests of bluebirds are tidy and homogenous in composition. The lining is not distinctly separate from the base.

The female often finishes nest-building in five or six days. A bluebird in a hurry can complete a nest in as little as two days, while others stretch the task out over two weeks. Weather, the time of year, the size of the cavity and the availability of materials all affect how rapidly the job goes. The nest is a cup proportioned like a shallow shaving mug. The interior of the cup is 2 3/8 inches in diameter and about 2 1/4 inches deep. The female builds up the nest until it is close enough to the cavity opening for convenient feeding of the young, about three inches

***People sometimes use really deep nest boxes because they want bluebirds to nest way down below the entry hole, where predators can't get at them. But deep boxes don't add up to safety; they just make bluebirds build higher nests until they get close to the hole. I don't see the point of forcing the birds to fill up a huge cavity. There are better ways of dealing with predators than that.***

*Opposite: An open mouth inside asks to be fed this big grasshopper.*

*– Dick Peterson Photo*

***Tree swallow nests look different because they use so many feathers, but they're the right size and shape for bluebirds. I've seen bluebirds chase tree swallows away from a box and then simply use the swallows' nest to raise their own young.***

*Preceding Spread: Nesting begins when the female accepts one of the cavities her mate has located.*

*– Bill Marchel Photo*

***Do bluebirds cooperate with each other much more than other birds do, or are their "selfless" acts simply witnessed more often because of how closely humans observe bluebirds? We don't know. But bluebirds are remarkably social and cooperative.***

below the opening. Bluebirds do not build a nest up to any certain height; they "measure down from the hole," in the phrase of some observers.

The female then begins laying eggs at the rate of one a day until three to seven eggs have been laid. The most common range is four to six eggs. Veteran bluebirders claim the typical number once was six but now is five. (If that is true, nobody can explain why the number has dropped.) Egg-laying typically takes five days.

Observers have attempted to identify the variables that affect clutch size. The size of the nesting cavity is not important; bluebirds in a roomy cavity lay no more eggs than bluebirds in a confined cavity. Clutch size is affected by the maturity of the female. Young females raising their first broods usually lay four eggs in the first nesting of the season.Older females more often lay five. The second or third nestings of the season are likely to have fewer eggs. Bluebird eggs are slightly smaller than robin eggs but otherwise quite similar in appearance. While bluebird eggs are usually a "robin's egg blue" color, white eggs are not uncommon.

Incubation usually begins five days after egg-laying starts. Brooding is done exclusively by the female. Only she has the brood patch, a featherless area on her breast that transfers warmth to the eggs. Incubation begins after all eggs have been laid, assuring that all eggs are warmed equally and will hatch at the same time. If the female has to leave the nest, the male might sit on the eggs temporarily to guard them and protect them against chilling.

The ideal brooding temperature is about 98° F. Eggs can be cooled briefly without losing viability. A more dangerous problem is high temperatures, as some manmade nest boxes get dangerously hot. The maximum temperature the eggs can survive is 107° F. Lethal temperatures prevail in some houses when the outside temperature is only 87° F. Incubation takes about 14 days for a first brood, 13 days for a second. Warmer summer temperatures may account for the difference. About 65 percent of the eggs hatch.

Bluebirds attempt at least two nestings per year. Authorities used to say many pairs nested three times a year, but most observers now believe bluebirds seen

## FIGURE 1

Following is a list of fruit-bearing trees that can be planted to attract bluebirds and other wildlife and to supplement their diets of insects and other food sources.

| Summer and Autumn Bearing Fruit Trees | Winter Bearing Fruit Trees |
|---|---|
| American Elderberry | Red Chokeberry |
| Scarlet Elderberry | Spicebush |
| Service Berry | Bittersweet |
| Tatarian Honeysuckle | Hackberry |
| European Mountain Ash | Flowering Dogwood |
| Flowering Crab | Small-leaved Cotoncaster |
| Common Buckthorn | Washington Hawthorn |
| Mapleleaf Viburnum | Blackthorn |
| Hobblebush | Inkberry, Pokeweed |
| Nannyberry | Smooth Winterberry |
| Siebold Viburum | American Holly |
| Witherod | Black Alder |
| Alternate-leaf Dogwood | Western Red Cedar |
| Silky Dogwood | Privet |
| Gray Dogwood | Amur Honeysuckle |
| Roundleaf Dogwood | Moonseed |
| Red-osier Dogwood | Bayberry |
| Cornelian Cherry | Sour Gum |
| Kousa Dogwood | Virginia Creeper |
| Common Snowberry | Pyracantha |
| Highbush Blueberry | Small Sumac |
| Black Huckleberry | Smooth Sumac |
| Wild Blackberry | Staghorn Sumac |
| Japanese Barberry | Multiflora Rose |
| Pin Cherry | Mountain Ash |
| Common Chokeberry | Coralberry |
| Black Cherry | High-bush Cranberry |
| Red Mulberry | Blackhaw |
| White Mulberry | Red Cedar |
| Russian Olive | |
| Autumn Olive | |
| Asiatic Sweetleaf | |
| Greenbrier | |
| Wild Grape | |
| Arrowwood | |
| Lowbush Blueberry | |

***I've seen the ideal temperature for nestlings listed at 95° F, but think that is too low. I once shooed a female off her eggs and quickly inserted an accurate thermometer in the nest. It read 98° F. If anything, the ideal is slightly higher than that.***

nesting late in summer are actually working on their second brood, not their third. These would be birds that had an earlier nesting effort destroyed by weather or predation. If bluebirds do nest successfully a third time, it would more likely happen in southern states with a longer potential nesting season.

When the baby bluebirds emerge from the eggs, the female either removes the broken shells from the nest or consumes them herself. Bluebirds are always tidy housekeepers.

The female continues to brood the near-naked nestlings. Very susceptible to cold, baby bluebirds sometimes die of hypothermia if a driving rain enters the cavity. The warmth of their mother normally brings the nestlings through this critical period. The female broods the young almost constantly for nearly a week while they develop feathers to conserve their own heat. The male brings food both to his mate and the nestlings during this time.

NESTLINGS

Newborn bluebirds are about as ugly as they one day will be beautiful. They are shaped like bowling pins with fat heads and ungainly leg and wing appendages. Almost entirely naked, the wild mop of dark fuzz on the babies' heads just adds to the homely effect. Their eyes are shut and covered by thin skin through which the bulging, bluish eyes are visible.

Baby bluebirds are altricial, meaning they are born nearly naked. Robins and other birds with nests exposed to the open air are born wearing more protective feathering than bluebirds. But though young bluebirds seem at a disadvantage in this respect, their cavities and the care of their mother combines to give them a higher survival rate than nestlings hatched in conventional nests.

The main feature of the babies, particularly from the perspective of their parents, is their huge mouth. As soon as they've fought free of the egg, baby bluebirds present gaping, beseeching mouths to the adults. The adults share equally the task of feeding the young, another example of the many ways bluebirds seem to be "model citizens."

It is also common for the young of a previous nesting to help feed the babies of their parents' second nesting.

*Opposite: Removing a fecal sac.*

*– Dick Peterson Photo*

***I cannot prove beyond doubt that a bluebird pair has nested three times in one year. Many times I have seen them bring two broods off, prepare a third nest and lay an egg or two in it and then abandon it. Once I saw a pair of bluebirds feeding young on October 4. We later found those babies dead in the nest.***

*Opposite: Four nestlings is a fairly common number.*

*– Steve Maslowski Photo*

Though they are little spotty-breasted youngsters, barely old enough to find their own food, they feed the new babies with the concern of a parent.

This kind of social cooperation is called "altruism" by some biologists and an example of "selfless genes" by others. Biologists believe cooperative behavior helps a species survive, yet the degree of selfless behavior in bluebirds challenges the usual notions of how far an individual will extend itself to support the good of the entire species.

The parents know no rest while the babies develop. The adults run a non-stop shuttle between the nest and the fields where they hunt insects. One parent or the other arrives with food about every five minutes, starting at dawn and continuing until sunset or even minutes beyond. Bluebird nestlings from a first nesting have their greatest need for food at that time of year when insects of all sorts are most plentiful. That is surely not a coincidence. The high demand of the whole bluebird family for food requires an abundance of insect life.

Each nestling in a brood of four gets a meal at roughly 20-minute intervals. An observer can judge the number of babies by the number of trips made by the adults, since each baby gets fed once every 20 minutes. Nestlings can survive without food for about a day, though any absence of the parents for several hours probably means they have been killed one way or another. At first, the adults mostly feed soft grubs or caterpillars to the young. As the babies

***I have a federal license to raise orphaned birds, which is an activity only for people very experienced with birds. I had two orphans, one about 33 days old and the other about 15 days old. One morning my wife looked in the cage where they both were and saw the older one beating up a mealworm. Then it went over to the little one and offered it, and the little one took it! Now, how did they learn that? This kind of work brings me joy I just can't express.***

*When unseasonably cold weather strikes in late winter or early spring, bluebirds can die, but they cope well for short periods. They sometimes huddle together in groups in nest boxes.*

mature, they receive larger and crunchier insects, primarily grasshoppers and crickets.

Bluebirds may adjust feeding intervals to allow their young to mature at the same time, even though some nestlings might have gotten a "head-start" on life. High temperatures at egg-laying time can cause eggs laid earlier to hatch prematurely, just as if they had been incubated earlier. Yet these early-hatching young reach full size at the same time as their later-hatching brothers and sisters. The parents probably feed smaller babies more often to allow them to catch up with their larger siblings.

The young birds develop rapidly. Their eyes begin opening at about the eighth day. That provides one way of aging baby bluebirds. At 10 days, the pin feathers of the wing primaries just begin erupting through the quill. When the outer wing primaries are half an inch long, the box should not be opened anymore. The nestlings are almost old enough to become fledglings. If alarmed, they might leave the box prematurely.

To keep the nest clean, the parents periodically remove the waste of their young.The white pellets of excreta are encapsulated in a thin membrane that resembles a little polyethylene bag. The adults carry these fecal sacs some distance (10 to 80 feet) from the nest before depositing them. This keeps odors around the nest itself at a minimum, possibly making it less likely that predators with keen noses will locate an easy meal. Bluebird nest hygiene sometimes becomes a little more casual close to the time the nestlings are ready to leave the nest.

The young can *fledge* – fly from the nest – anywhere from 17 to 21 days after birth.That fairly broad span reflects the variables of weather and food availability, which in turn determine how quickly the babies develop. The young birds are called and teased out of the security of their cavity by their parents. Most often, the youngsters take flight for the first time 17 or 18 days after being born. Occasionally a fledgling is too weak or timid to leave the nesting box with its siblings. After several hours of coaxing, the parents abandon such birds, and they eventually die in the nesting cavity. They were not up to one of life's first challenges and probably would not have been up to subsequent ones.

*Top: A bluebird clutch rarely includes this many eggs.*

– Dick Peterson Photo

*Bottom: About seven percent of bluebirds lay white eggs.*

– Dick Peterson Photo

Most make it. With no previous experience, the young bluebirds are able to fly in their very first attempt. They land in the branches of trees or shrubs off the ground. They often then work their way higher in the tree, calling to let their parents know just where they are.

In this respect, bluebirds and other cavity-nesting birds differ from birds that nest in the open. For example, baby robins on their first flight from the nest usually flutter to the ground, where they are highly vulnerable to predation. Cavity-nesters leave the security of the nesting area for the relative security of branches out of the reach of ground-based predators.

The initial flight of the fledglings might be as long as 100 feet, the range depending on the proximity of a secure place to land. Longer flights are possible for fledglings flying with a tailwind. That first flight is a pivotal and irrevocable event in a bluebird's life. Once they leave the protection of the nesting cavity, they will not return. If forcibly placed back in the nest by a person who knows they have left prematurely, the young leave again as soon as they can. They will not enter a nesting cavity again until they are mature and ready to raise a family of their own.

The fledglings then are fed, defended and tended by their parents. The whole bluebird family huddles together on cold nights to share warmth. Both adults continue to offer food to the fledglings for a few more days. Then the female turns her attention to her second nesting effort. The male takes over the feeding of the young. After about two weeks of instruction, the fledglings are entirely capable of fending for themselves. After another week they might be assisting in the feeding of the second batch of nestlings. The young are fully independent 35 to 40 days after birth.

The same two adults usually mate again to produce the second brood, but not always. The male might mate with another female while his first partner is brooding the first clutch. Under ideal circumstances, a bluebird pair might bring a dozen young bluebirds into the world in one nesting season. But, circumstances are rarely ideal. Bluebirds need considerable help from us.

*Opposite: Bluebird fledglings, with the spots typical of juvenile thrushes.*

*– Steve Maslowski Photo*

***Examples of bluebird "altruism" are numerous. It is common for fledglings barely old enough to care for themselves to feed the nestlings of their parents second brood. According to one report, a one-year-old male bluebird raised a brood of his own, then moved to his parents' box to help them feed their new brood. If bluebird fledglings wander into the territory of another bluebird family, the adults won't chase them off. They feed them.***

# The Rise and Fall of Bluebirds

To describe the history of eastern bluebird populations in North America, we have to do a little speculation. There simply are not enough "hard" facts about this part of the bluebirds' story.

*Spread Pages 58-59: Bluebirds emerging from the eggs.*

*– Dick Peterson Photo*

*Opposite: The primary feeding tactics of bluebirds is perching until they spot an insect.*

*– Ted Thousand Photo*

ORIGINAL ABUNDANCE

Most people assume bluebirds in pre-settlement North America were quite abundant. It's a dangerous assumption. Not much of eastern North America would have been ideal bluebird habitat until after European settlers began changing the land. Between the eastern seaboard and the prairies of the midwest lay a vast forest called by many "The Big Woods." Though there would have been oak-savannah openings and natural fire clearings, this ancient forest had few of the sunny openings bluebirds require. Of course, bluebirds would not have lacked for cavities. Food, however, would have been a limiting factor.

It is a good guess – but only that – that the eastern bluebird peaked in numbers sometime in the second half of the 19th century. Most towns of that era were small, with developed areas adjoined by vacant lots, creating a checkerboard of varied habitat. The Big Woods had been chopped up but not chopped down.

The eastern half of North America in the 1800s was mostly given over to small farms with little fields and great habitat diversity. Those farms had a great many scattered woodlots full of old trees where cavity-nesting birds could rear their young. Even the timber fenceposts of the time had cavities that afforded bluebirds a place to rear their young.

No data exists to tell us just how abundant bluebirds were. There are accounts of migrating flocks of "hundreds" of bluebirds. The frequent appearance of bluebirds in songs, literature and art suggests they were very frequently seen. By some accounts, bluebirds were once "as common as robins." We'll never know any numbers.

## THE DECLINE

It is impossible to document their decline with precision. Yet there is no doubt that bluebirds have fallen on difficult times in the current century. The decline wasn't caused by a single, dramatic event.

Dr. Thomas Musselman of Quincy, Illinois, is generally regarded as the father of the bluebird recovery program. He invented the concept of a "bluebird trail" – a series of five or more nest boxes erected along a trail for convenient monitoring. Musselman worked for decades to educate people about the plight of the bluebird. Musselman's influence continues to this day, as people he motivated to work for bluebirds went on to motivate others.

Among them, none has been more eloquent and ultimately influential than Dr. Lawrence Zeleny. His "Bluebird Trail" columns in *Nature Society News* reached countless readers. Following his retirement in 1966, Zeleny turned his energies to sounding the alarm about falling bluebird populations. One result was his book, **The Bluebird**. Published in 1976, it is still in print and still motivating people to help arrest the decline.

Zeleny wrote that bluebird populations "declined drastically" from the late 1920s to the late 1970s. He estimated that eastern bluebird populations decreased by 90 percent over that period. Such a trend would threaten the continued existence of the eastern bluebird. Zeleny based those estimates on his own recollections and those of other friends of bluebirds who had lived long enough to see disturbing changes in their populations.

Beginning in 1966, the U.S. Fish and Wildlife Service has conducted a comprehensive annual North American Breeding Bird Survey (BBS). A paper written in 1990 by John R. Sauer and Sam Droege attempted to define trends in the BBS data. That data documented widespread bluebird declines in the 1966-1978 period. "Extreme local declines" followed the especially severe winters of 1976-1977 and 1977-1978. Then, from 1978-1987, eastern bluebird populations increased in almost every region covered by the survey. Those improvements brought bluebird numbers back very close to the earliest BBS figures.

*Opposite: Bluebirds suffer when storms make insects unavailable to them.*

*– Steve Kirkpatrick Photo*

***I put up my first bluebird house in 1918 in Minneapolis, near the University of Minnesota. In those days it was still fairly common to see bluebirds in the residential districts of cities. If you put houses up, you expected to get bluebirds. But bluebirds were already having trouble with sparrows.***

*– Lawrence Zeleny*

## FIGURE 2

## THE PETERSON IN-BOX SPARROW TRAP

This diagram illustrates the basic configuration and positioning of the Peterson Sparrow Trap. Full-scale plans are available from the Bluebird Recovery Program (BBRP). See Appendix for more information.

**Note:** Sparrow and starling traps, whether in-box or ground types, should never be left untended. They could cause the death of beneficial birds.

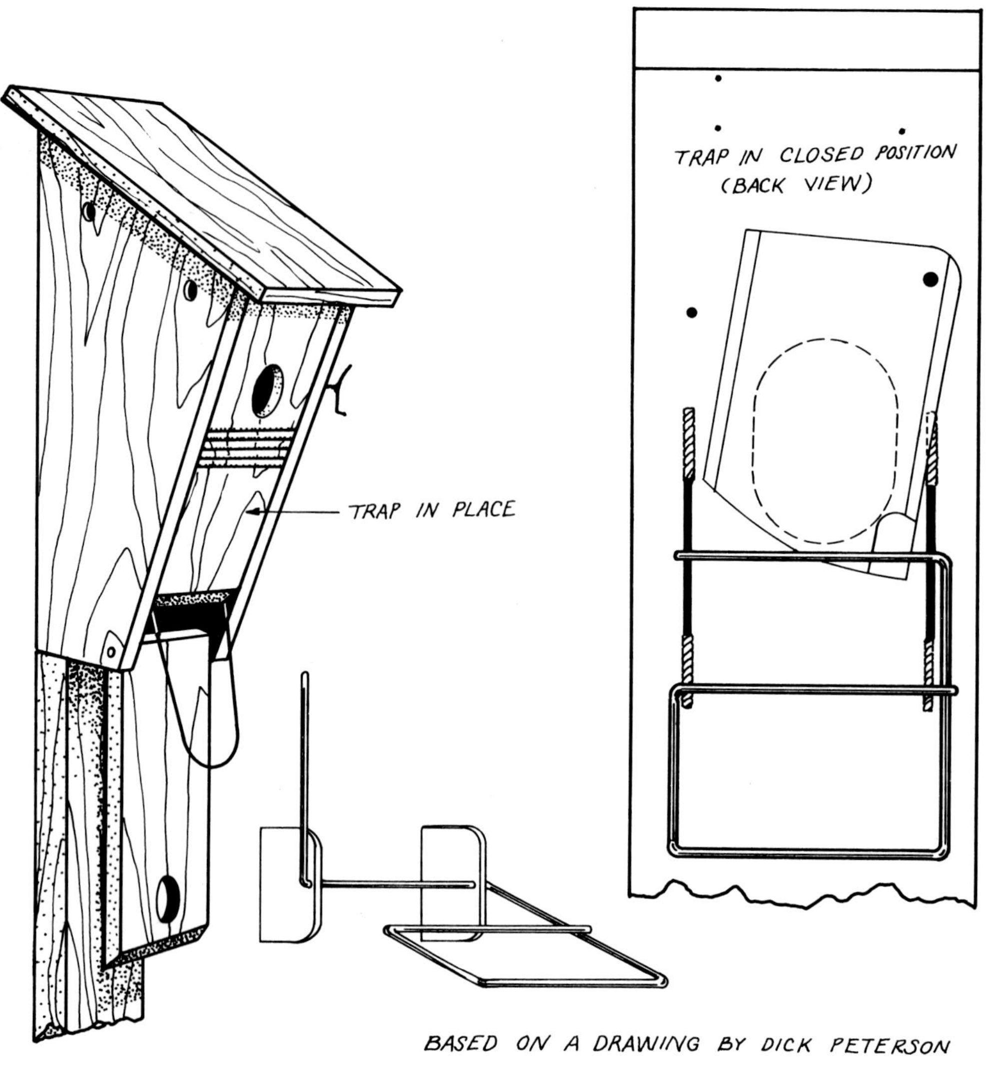

*Preceding Page: Flying squirrels are among the many animals that make use of cavities.*

*– Steve Maslowski Photo*

*Opposite: Most bluebird eggs are "robin's egg blue."*

*– Dick Peterson Photo*

***The North American Bluebird Society received a tremendous boost in the early days from a magazine story about the plight of bluebirds. The article appeared in Parade, the magazine inserted in millions of Sunday newspapers across the country. It invited concerned people to send a quarter to NABS. That appeal generated 80,000 letters! Almost overnight, we had a long list of interested people and an operating fund of $20,000.***

*– Lawrence Zeleny*

What had caused the decline and subsequent recovery? Sauer and Droege's analysis suggested "climatic events" – in other words, weather – as the most significant factor. Bluebirds were hurt by exceptionally bitter winters, they argued, then returned to normal levels when a period of more typical weather prevailed.

Of course, the documented rebound of bluebird numbers in the late 1970s and 1980s also coincides with the surge of the bluebird conservation movement. That movement motivated bluebird fans to erect nest boxes from which countless thousand bluebirds fledged.

Since we cannot now go back and conduct accurate surveys of the bluebird populations that existed decades or centuries ago, we cannot document bluebird population fluctuations with certainty. If the recollections of long-time bird lovers are not "hard" data, they are nevertheless the best data we have.

There is a consensus of scientific opinion that bluebirds declined throughout the 20th century, reaching an all-time low in the late 1970s. They are doing better now, though obviously in need of all the support we can give.

## CAUSES FOR DECLINE

The reasons bluebirds have declined are much easier to identify, but even on this topic, there is confusion about which factors have hurt bluebirds most severely.

An example is uncertainty about the role of persistent pesticides. Biologists and bluebird fans know these chemicals hurt bluebirds indirectly (by diminishing the food supply) and directly (by poisoning bluebirds). What nobody knows is exactly how harmful toxic chemicals have been.

Unquestionably, loss of habitat has taken a terrible toll on bluebirds. Urban development and intensive agriculture have destroyed an enormous amount of former habitat. Habitat destruction has taken two forms: elimination of desirable bluebird habitat and of nesting cavities.

The general loss of bluebird habitat has deprived bluebirds of the mix of trees and sunny grasslands they require. Woodlots have been cleared. When small farms were replaced by large ones, patchwork fields with grassy

*Opposite: This bluebird sits on an unusual perch: a cattail.*

*– Steve Kirkpatrick Photo*

***I think bluebirds have not just recovered but have extended their range in areas where there are now bluebird houses. My old friend, Carl Tinquist, recently died at the age of 102. He told me he had never seen a bluebird on his land from 1912 until I put houses there.***

corners gave way to vast acreages of monoculture row crops. Urban development and highway construction caused enormous amounts of bluebird habitat to disappear forever under acres of concrete and asphalt.

Cavity-nesters like bluebirds depend upon trees with dead limbs or dead trees that are still standing. Both have been disappearing. Dead trees are now routinely cut up for firewood or removed simply because they strike people as unattractive. People even take the trouble to saw dead limbs off living trees because they are "unsightly."

These massive, pervasive habitat changes may have limited bluebird numbers more than anything else. Many observers also blame two interlopers that have bedeviled bluebirds ever since they were introduced to North America. The alien house sparrow and European starling have wreaked havoc on bluebird populations.

The bird, once called the English sparrow and now known as the house sparrow, was introduced to this country in 1851 and 1852. Not a sparrow at all, but a weaver finch, *Passer domesticus* spread so quickly from town to town and farm to farm that it overran the country within five decades. That is hardly surprising. The house sparrow is regarded as the most abundant and successful wild bird species in the world. Noisy and aggressive, the house sparrow is clever at using human buildings and human waste to its advantage.

House sparrows are the most serious avian threat and the single most pernicious enemy of bluebirds. House sparrows claim bluebird houses and then violently defend them. If bluebirds set up in a house claimed by sparrows, the sparrows evict or destroy them. Sparrows have a sharp beak that efficiently pierces the head of adult bluebirds or their eggs. Nobody has yet devised a way to keep sparrows out of bluebird houses because sparrows can enter any cavity that bluebirds can.

The European starling, *Sturnus vulgaris*, is one of those birds that carries an appropriate-sounding Latin name. According to legend, starlings were introduced into New York's Central Park in 1890 by someone who wanted America to have every bird represented in Shakespeare's literature. It is a sad, ironic twist that some scholars think Shakespeare's reference to "starlings" was a mistake. He might have meant another bird.

*Preceding Spread: When paper wasps begin building nests in bluebird boxes, you want to act quickly.*

*– Dick Peterson Photo*

*Opposite: Bringing in food for the nestlings.*

*– Steve Maslowski Photo*

Regardless, from 60 individuals, starling numbers have swollen to over 200 million. In fact, starlings continue to expand their range, having only recently established themselves in western states. Starlings first thrived in cities, but have flooded into rural areas in recent decades. There they compete with bluebirds, who have retreated to wilder areas since the sparrow took over towns.

Large and aggressive, the starling is a bully that no bluebird can handle. When a starling and bluebird compete for a nesting site, the starling wins every time. Starlings routinely kill or evict baby bluebirds from a nest cavity. Starlings now consume a large share of the winter food needed by bluebirds at a crucial time of the year, just before they migrate north to nest.

The impact of these alien species on bluebirds has been devastating. Now starlings threaten woodpeckers, which indirectly adds to the damage starlings are doing to bluebirds. Downy, hairy, red-headed and red-bellied woodpeckers are declining because starlings are usurping their nest cavities. Without woodpeckers, bluebirds will find even fewer natural cavities in the future.

Another villain contributing to the decline of bluebird populations is the common house cat. Cat numbers have expanded as human populations have expanded. Cats often become clever and skillful bluebird predators. Any reasonably fit cat can leap over four feet, which means cats can jump to the height of many bluebird houses, even without climbing a pole. They then reach in the hole with needle-sharp claws and drag out any bluebirds within.

Another threat is the cat's ability to prey on bluebirds away from the nest box. Many cats learn to loll about on the ground near a bluebird house, feigning indifference while bluebirds dive-bomb them to drive them away. Eventually a bluebird comes too close and gets swiped out of the air. Predation blamed on raccoons is often caused by cats. Because of the affection so many people have for cats, the full significance of their damage is rarely acknowledged.

As mentioned, chemical sprays have played a role in the decline of bluebirds.Bluebird trail monitors often witness these impacts, albeit on a small scale. Bluebirds often disappear when pesticides are sprayed near a nest box, sometimes abandoning eggs. Bluebird trail monitors

## FIGURE 3

## THE JIM NOEL WIRE COON GUARD

This diagram illustrates materials and measurements for constructing a wire mesh coon guard for attachment on this front of bluebird nesting boxes. This predator trap is discussed at greater length in later chapters of this text.

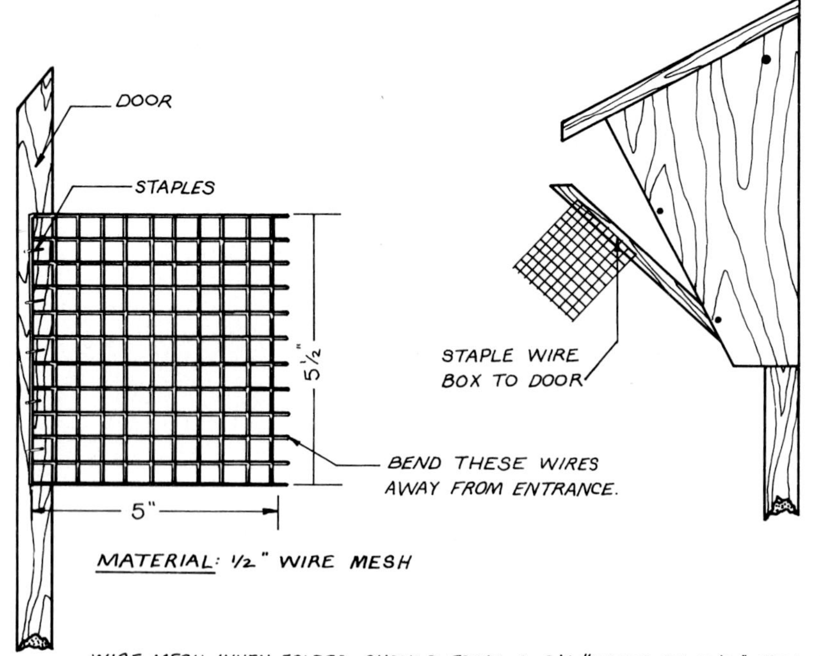


WIRE MESH, WHEN FOLDED, SHOULD FORM A 3½" WIDE BY 5½" TALL BOX.

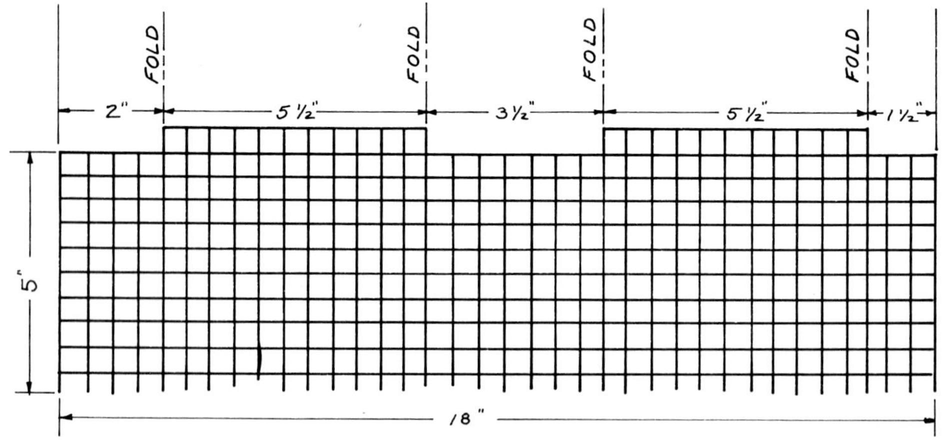

occasionally find dead or dying adult bluebirds, the apparent victims of pesticide poisoning. Sprays now make two former prime bluebird habitats unusable. Orchards and golf courses once offered bluebirds ideal habitat. Now bluebirds fare poorly in these areas because many orchards and golf courses are soaked with deadly chemicals.

The overall picture is sobering. If our society viewed bluebirds as pests that needed to be eradicated, we might do exactly what we have done. That is, we would deprive them of food, destroy their nesting habitat and introduce predatory competitors (a big one and a small one) to make it hazardous for bluebirds to use the few cavities left.

*When I began to be interested in bluebirds, the only man I could find who was successful at raising them refused to tell me how. He said, "Sonny, it took me a lifetime to learn how to raise bluebirds. And if you're really serious about helping the bluebird, you're going to have to do it the way I did." I came away with the determination that nobody would get that kind of answer if they sought help from me.*

## RECOVERY

Up to this point, the story of the bluebird is a very familiar and tragic one. Habitat eradication, toxic chemicals and competition from alien species have hurt many other species, too. But what is different about bluebirds is how much people cared about their plight. Many Americans have worked to make sure the sun never rises over this land without bluebirds being there to welcome it.

Again, there isn't much hard information to prove that bluebirds have rebounded or that nesting boxes have been important in that effort. The BBS data proves a resurgence of bluebirds following the disastrous winters of the late 1970s. Beyond that, we only have the reports of concerned observers to show that bluebirds are recovering.

Yet the weight of that evidence clearly suggests that bluebirds are responding to the help people offer them. It might only be "anecdotal" information, but there is an overwhelming amount of it. People are seeing bluebirds where bluebirds have not been seen in decades. Bluebirds are even showing up where they never used to occur. People who have lived 70 years without seeing a single bluebird now see them frequently. Wildlife professionals agree with bluebird fans that the return of the bluebird is one of the great success stories in modern conservation.

The deepening concern of bluebird fans began to come to the public attention about two decades ago. An article in the June, 1977, *National Geographic* dramatized the bluebird's problems to the whole world. Dr. Lawrence

Zeleny's book on bluebirds appeared in 1976. It depicted the disturbing plight of the bluebird.

In 1978, Zeleny's efforts resulted in the creation of the North American Bluebird Society (NABS). That society has functioned since as the central source of information and coordination for bluebird recovery efforts in North America. Today NABS has about 5,000 members.

**Bluebirds!** co-author, Dick Peterson, of Brooklyn Center, Minnesota, began working seriously on bluebird recovery about 1960. His efforts prompted the Minnesota Chapter of the Audubon Society to organize the Bluebird Recovery Program. Minnesota's program has become a model for efforts in other states, including a vigorous program in Wisconsin.Membership in Minnesota's program currently stands near 4,000.

The pioneers of the bluebird recovery program had to learn the basics of bluebird conservation. It wasn't easy. Bluebird numbers were so low it was difficult to attract a breeding pair to a nest box. There was a lot of heartbreak in the early years, too, because the bluebirders lacked the experience and technology to keep their bluebirds safe from predators. However, they laid the foundation for the success of current efforts.

Two keys to the success of bluebird recovery programs have been experimentation and the sharing of information. The work is far from over. But if today's bluebird fans still have to contend with blowflies, raccoons, starlings and sparrows, they at least don't have to contend with a lack of information.

We now know what needs to be done. What remains is finding enough concerned, responsible people to further the good work that has been advanced so far.

*Opposite: A bluebird preening. Bluebirds are neat and clean in all ways.*

*– Steve Maslowski Photo*

***People who love cats and insist on giving them some outdoor freedom can go a long way toward preventing damage to birds in their area. Just trim the claws with ordinary clippers. This won't harm the cat and will prevent its snagging birds in the air and reduce its ability to climb.***

## FIGURE 4

## JENSEN-ARNDT "COOLIE HAT" COON GUARDS

This diagram illustrates measurements and materials for the fabrication of sheet metal "coolie hat" coon guards for use on wooden and steel posts that support nesting boxes. The peculiar name derives from the shape of the coon guard when it's wrapped around a post.

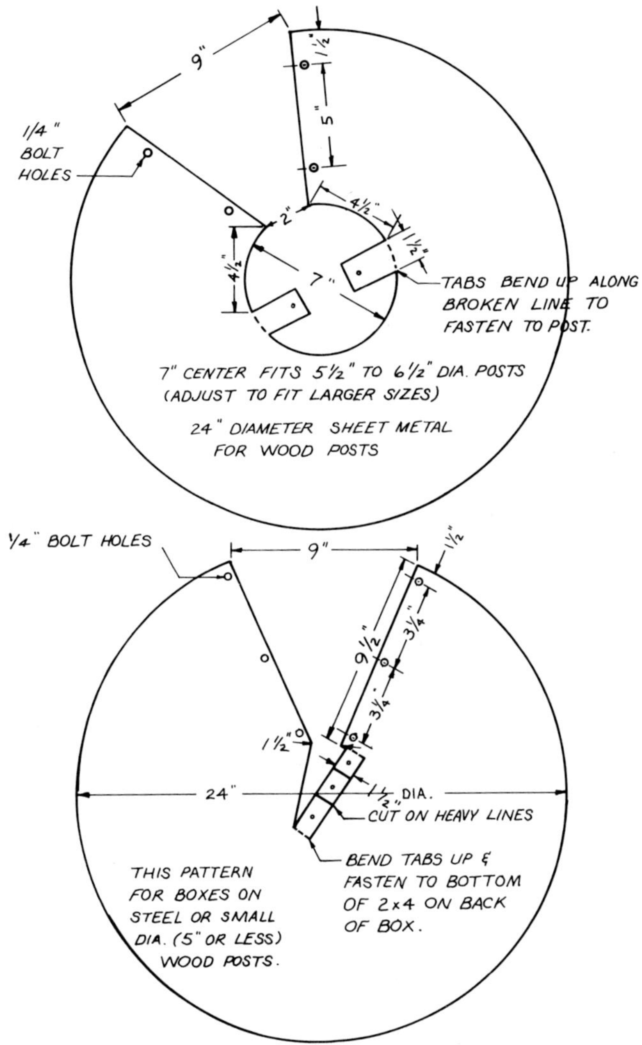


*Opposite: If it itches, scratch it!*

*– Steve Maslowski Photo*

*Following Spread: Nestlings are fed from dawn to dusk, each bird receiving food every 20 minutes.*

*– Dick Peterson Photo*

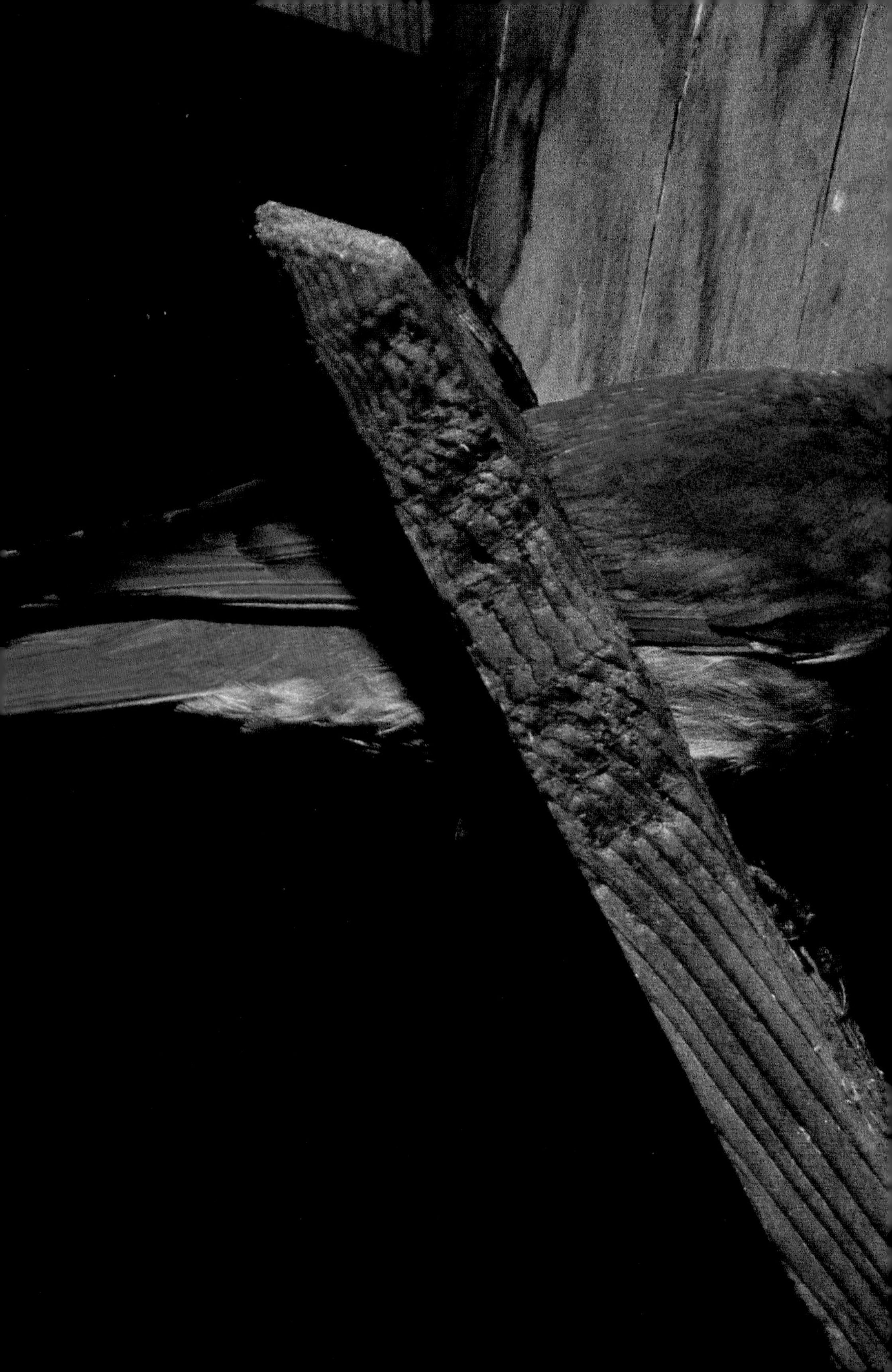

*Opposite: This nestling is probably impatient for its next meal.*

*– Steve Maslowski Photo*

*Above: As one parent leaves, the other arrives with more food.*

*– Steve Maslowski Photo*

Seed Potatoes

# Bluebirds and You

Would you like to help the eastern bluebird? You can choose from among several bluebird conservation efforts and programs.

The most appropriate first step is to contact other people who are already deeply involved. Membership in bluebird conservation groups is inexpensive and extremely useful. The national group is the North American Bluebird Society (NABS). Their quarterly publication, *Sialia*, is an excellent publication. It documents the latest thinking about bluebird conservation. NABS conducts local and national meetings on bluebird conservation, and NABS members receive merchandise offers and plans for building nest boxes. Above all, membership gives you access to experienced and enthusiastic bluebirders.

Many, but not all, states in the range of the eastern bluebird also have local bluebird recovery groups. The problems facing bluebirds differ from region to region. If you are a beginning bluebirder, the most useful tips often come from the most experienced friends of bluebirds in your area. You can gain the benefit of their wisdom by joining the local bluebird recovery group. If you don't know how to contact that group, your state natural resources agency will have the information.

Most people want to do more than join groups. They want to become directly involved in personal bluebird conservation.

Again, there are several ways to proceed. You can feed bluebirds, which is especially important in winter and at nesting time. You can aid wintering bluebirds by putting out roost boxes that give them shelter and warmth on bitter nights. You might be able to contribute to efforts to survey local populations.

FEEDING

Feeding bluebirds gives you a great chance to enjoy them, as the birds will come eagerly to feeders and give you many chances to observe them. It is a pleasure for the whole family.

*Opposite: John Rominsky with bluebird nestlings. Maintaining a bluebird trail is a wonderful hobby for all sorts of people.*

*– Dick Peterson Photo*

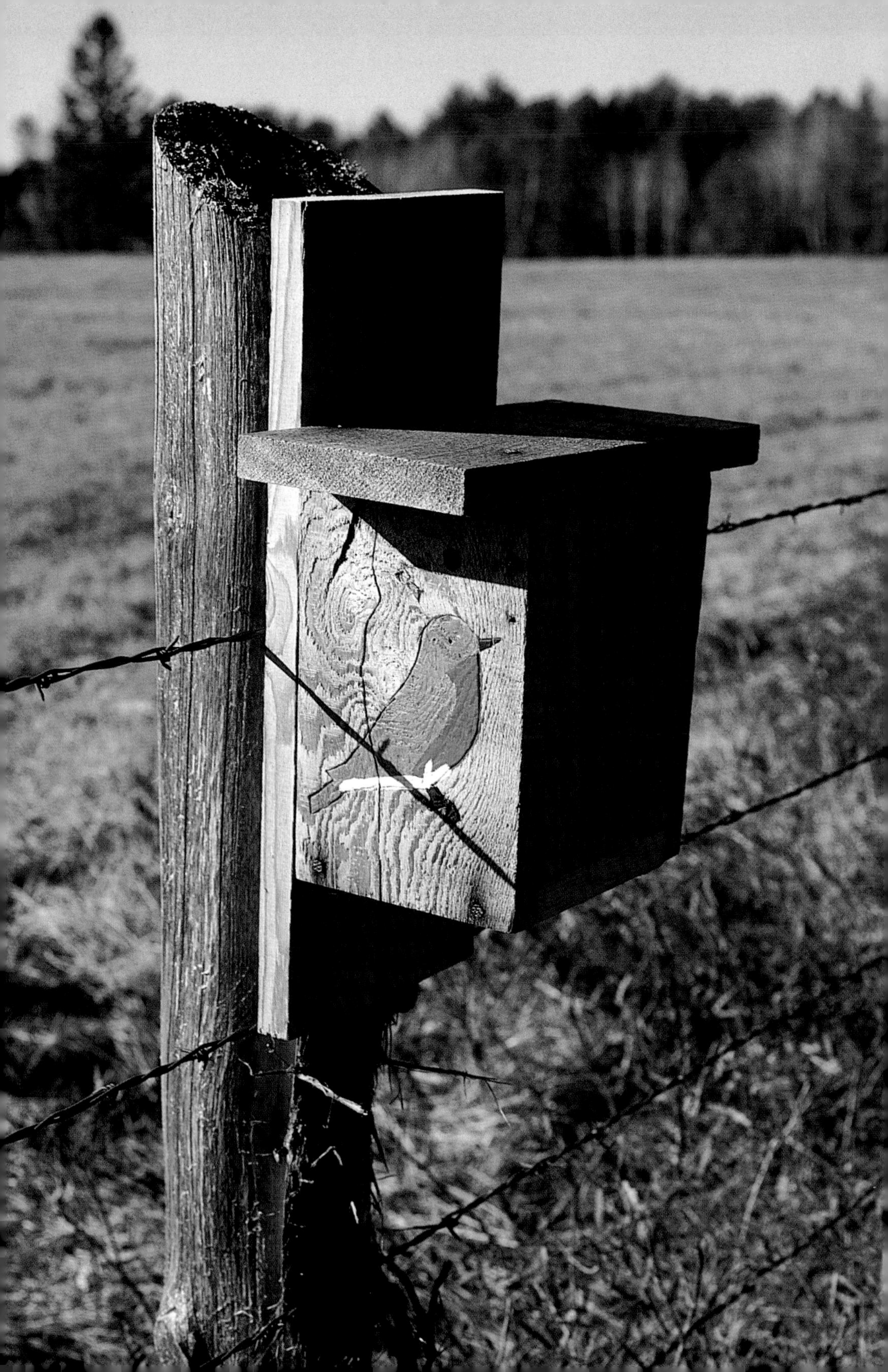

Feeding is seen as more important for bluebird survival than some people used to think. Although bluebirds eat many different types of food, they need a steady supply, particularly when the young are growing. An interruption in the availability of food for just three days in an area can mean that vast numbers of bluebirds die. Winter feeding helps bluebirds endure the stresses of migration and nesting in good physical condition.

Bluebirds seem to like stationary, not swinging, feeders. Tray or platform feeders work well, and they can be quite near human dwellings.

Mealworms are a wonderful food for bluebirds. They are sold inexpensively in many pet food stores. You can breed and maintain mealworms, keeping them in the basement in a flat box on a mealy medium which feeds and houses them. They are very easy to keep.

People who feed bluebirds often offer a combination of mealworms and food. One popular food is mixed from one part flour and three parts of cornmeal, with lard, peanut butter or peanut hearts added.

TRAILING

More than anything else, bluebirds need better opportunities to reproduce. This makes bluebird trailing the keystone program in modern bluebird conservation.

***Trails in areas with sparrows, raccoons or house cats need the most monitoring. Yet there are rural areas where predation of any sort is uncommon. For example, one couple put 30 boxes up on 200 acres of undeveloped recreational land. Though they aren't able to get to that land to monitor the boxes frequently, they've had only minor predation on two or three boxes in eight years. If they experienced more predation, they would make other arrangements. Meanwhile they are providing bluebirds with cavities.***

*Opposite: Not just a "bird-house," this box is obviously meant for bluebirds.*

*– Robert W. Baldwin Photo*

***"If you build it, they will come." Though the advice appears in a popular novel and movie, it applies well to bluebird houses. You might need to wait, and you might need to move your boxes around until you find the right area. It might takes years . . . or hours. But if you plan well, you will get bluebirds in your boxes.***

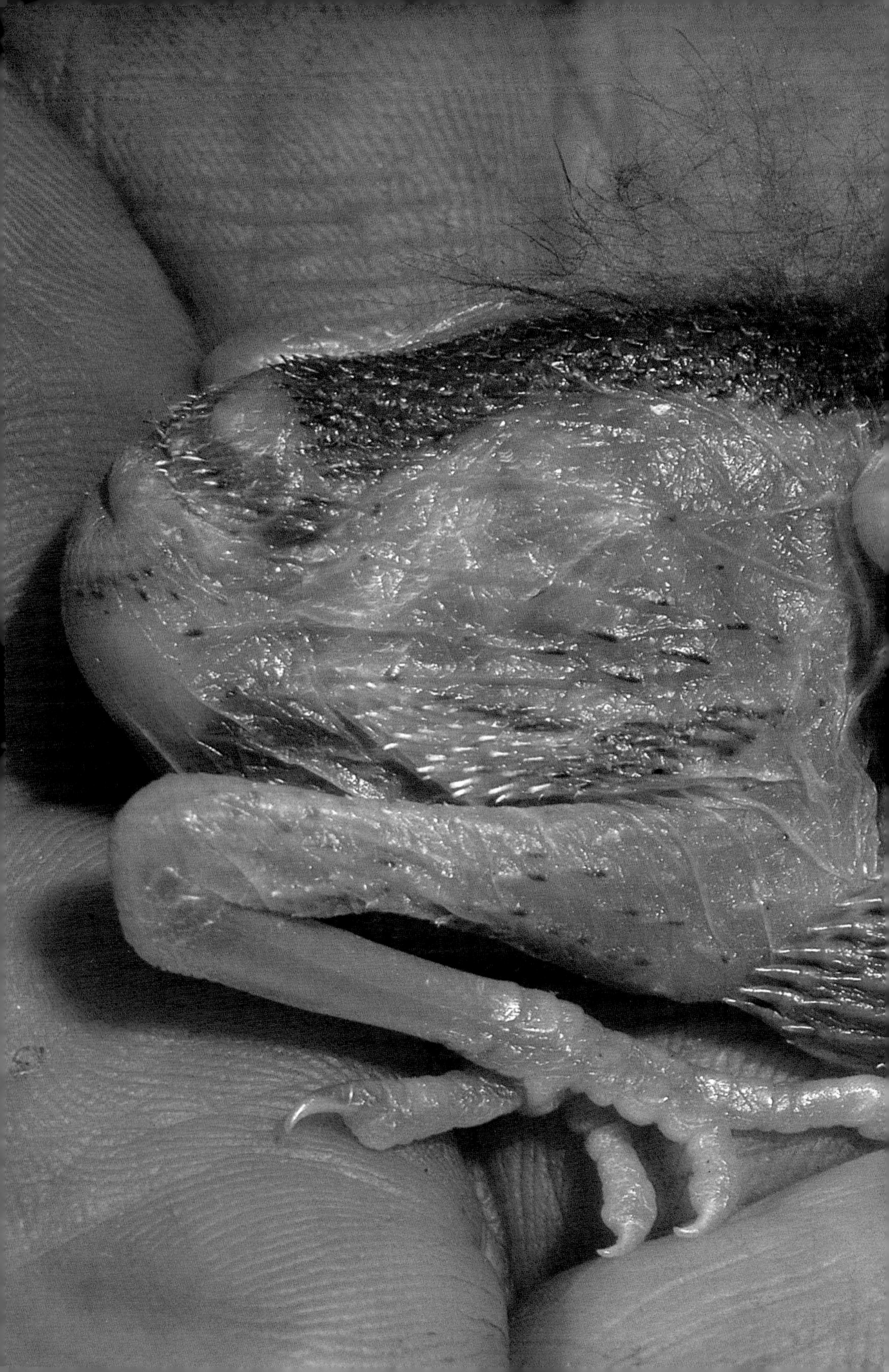

*Preceding Spread: These are seven days old, with wing primaries that have not yet erupted from the quill.*

*– Dick Peterson Photo*

Happily enough, it is also the most satisfying method of helping bluebirds. Setting up your own bluebird trail is neither expensive nor difficult. The only requirement is the commitment to try.

Trailing can be divided into three general activities. You start by acquiring boxes. Next, you scout out some suitable bluebird habitat where you can place them. Then you monitor what happens to those boxes, dealing with any problems that arise. The next three chapters will discuss each of these areas in some detail.

All these activities are important, but none so important as monitoring. Do not put out boxes unless you are willing and able to check. Unmonitored boxes can become death traps, resulting in the loss of one or both adults. You then will have done more harm than good to bluebirds, in spite of your good intentions.

There is no magic "right" interval for monitoring. In general the more often you get around to check your boxes, the better. Some trails require more supervision than others. You should check each box once a week, more frequently if possible. Monitoring should be maintained throughout the nesting season from April through August. Your initial monitoring should precede the earliest possible arrival of the birds. Monitoring less than once in two weeks allows sparrows to get in your boxes and bring off broods, and the last thing anybody needs is more sparrows!

Remember the importance of monitoring when you decide how many boxes to set out. Some retired couples

***For a while when bluebird numbers were so desperately low, I maintained a trail of about 472 houses. That was quite a job. We were just enslaved. We would take three days to run the trail, then a week and a half later we'd start all over again. We couldn't take a vacation for several years. We've cut back to 140 boxes now, but now we can afford to because there are so many more bluebirds.***

*Top: These are chickadee eggs.*

*– Dick Peterson Photo*

*Bottom: The small egg is normal. Every now and then, bluebirds lay "freak" large eggs.*

*– Dick Peterson Photo*

*Opposite: Vi Peterson with some of the distinctive boxes designed by her husband.*

*– Dick Peterson Photo*

*Spread Pages 94-95: The eastern bluebird, having fallen to dangerously low population levels, is recovering now.*

*– Ted Thousand Photo*

have trails with several hundred nest boxes. Busy suburbanites raising children might have just three or four boxes set up around their homes. If you are just beginning bluebird trailing, it makes sense to begin modestly. Put out a few boxes that you can tend frequently rather than a great many boxes you end up neglecting.

Keep careful records on what is happening on your trail. Precise information is not only interesting but a vital part of monitoring. For example, you want to determine which day nestlings emerge from the eggs so you later know when to avoid spooking them into leaving the box prematurely.

Record all pertinent information as you check each box. Give every box an identifying number. A small reporter's note pad is convenient for jotting down field notes, including such items as the date, the number of eggs or nestlings and any evidence of predation. Many bluebirders transfer field notes to home computers to create data bases that can help others. Managing a bluebird trail is a fascinating educational process. To some degree, each trail is unique. In fact, each year on the same trail is unique. Trailing will continually present you with new challenges and new rewards.

But have faith. If you plan thoughtfully, you will get bluebirds at your boxes. And if you monitor those houses and deal with problems, your houses will produce bluebirds. You then will be adding more and more bluebirds to a world that can use all the symbols of happiness it can get.

*Opposite: Bluebirds make a major effort to nest twice a year.*

*– Bill Marchel Photo*

*Above: You can handle nestlings without causing the adults to abandon them.*

*– Dick Peterson Photo*

*Above: Orphaned bluebirds can be raised by people who apply for federal permits.*

– Dick Peterson Photo

*Opposite: Bluebirds happily nest near apartment complexes if people don't harass them.*

– Dick Peterson Photo

# A Good Nest Box

Bluebird fans often become intrigued with the challenge of designing a better box: a box that is more functional for bluebirds, easier to check and more predator-proof. Bluebirds have benefitted enormously from all the scrutiny given to nest box design.

Those same efforts have given rise to sharp controversies about which nest box design is best. Nest box disputes have dissipated energies that would have been directly more productively toward conservation. At times, people who should have been working together for bluebirds have scrapped bitterly about nest boxes.

You want to expose "your" bluebirds to as few hazards as possible. Avoid cute commercial boxes, many of which are plastic, or the products of home handymen with uninformed notions of what a "birdhouse" should be. Such boxes are built by people who have never run a bluebird trail and who don't understand the special problems of bluebirds.The only nest boxes you should use are those approved by bluebird recovery groups. Local bluebird groups are excellent sources of guidance.

If you build your own nest boxes, use plans for boxes approved by bluebird conservationists. And follow the plans faithfully. Uninformed attempts to improve on them usually run into trouble. Consider building your first boxes from pre-cut kits. The Appendix lists sources for boxes, box plans and kits.

## THE BASICS OF NEST BOX DESIGN

Some matters are not controversial. A good box must offer protection against the elements. It should be insulated so the female can keep eggs and nestlings warm with her body heat. Drafty houses won't allow bluebirds to keep the eggs warm during early spring cold snaps.

Since excess heat can be a problem, nest boxes need sufficient ventilation and insulation so they won't "cook" the eggs on a hot afternoon. Quite a few types of boxes get dangerously hot. High air temperatures are less dangerous than pools of hot *still* air trapped in the boxes. Ventilation

*Opposite: Wild fruits and berries become very important to bluebirds from late fall to late spring.*

*– Steve Maslowski Photo*

***Houses should not be drafty from the bottom. I once found a bluebird incubating a full clutch of eggs on March 25. That early in the year, unless a bluebird has a cozy box, she can't keep it warm.***

above the nest is the key to safe temperature control.

To keep water out of the box, the entry and ventilation holes should be protected against wind-driven rains. There should be some provision for allowing any water entering the hole to drain away.

A good box must be easy to open for monitoring. Boxes that are awkward to check discourage people from checking them frequently.

The box should be as predator-proof as is practical. The entry hole must be too small to allow starlings to nest in the box. A bluebird box should never be equipped with a perch by the hole. Perches attract sparrows. Bluebirds can get a firm grip on the surface of a wood box. To help them, score the box front with a sharp tool right below the hole.

*Opposite: The Noel wire guard is the only guard proven a hundred percent successful against cats and raccoons.*

*– Steve Grooms Photo*

***In areas with high human vandalism, alert your local authorities. Inform them that it is a federal offense to meddle with the nesting of a protected bird.***

BOX MATERIALS

For all practical purposes, wood is the only appropriate building material at this time. Wood is a natural material with good insulating properties. Plastic houses often overheat. Some interesting experiments are being conducted with PVC plastic. That material cannot be endorsed yet, though it shows promise for the future.

Don't expose bluebirds to poisoning by using unsafe lumber. Green "pressure treated" lumber is impregnated with copper-arsenate as a preservative. If the chemical is not applied perfectly (and it often is not), the wood is toxic to bluebirds and humans. Exterior grade plywoods

***Bluebirds have nested in pockets in abandoned farm machinery, mailboxes, discarded cans, the grills of cars and in the mouths of ornamental cannons. If they can't find natural cavities, they'll use unnatural ones. Yet that does not mean "any old cavity will do." Birds using oddball cavities rarely succeed at fledging many of their young. What really counts is how many young fledge.***

*Opposite: No bird is more lovable or more dearly loved than the eastern bluebird.*

*– Dick Peterson Photo*

***If you paint your houses nicely, they blend in well and people find them attractive. You can put them up on properties where people would object to dumpy-looking boxes.***

*– Richard Hjort*

contain dangerously high levels of formaldehyde.

The premier wood is cedar. Cedar naturally resists deterioration when exposed to sun and rain. Weathered cedar is inconspicuous and attractive. Other supposedly weather-resistant woods, such as redwood and cyprus, cannot be counted on to last any longer than pine unless stained or painted. Douglas fir is the best second choice.

Never paint or stain the inside of a box. Natural, untreated wood is best. If you want to paint the exterior, close up the box and only paint what you can see. If you stain or paint the exterior of your box, you can choose from several types of wood materials. Pine, interior plywood and other inexpensive woods work well when weather-sealed. Use an exterior grade latex paint and give the top a second coat. A heavy grade of linseed oil stain works well, too.

Boxes should be a light color. The interiors of dark houses more readily reach lethally high temperatures. Lawrence Zeleny has determined that dark houses can run 12° F hotter than light boxes. Choose a light shade of such natural colors as green, tan or grey. Houses that blend in with their surroundings are more appealing than garish boxes and less likely to draw the attention of human vandals.

## THE ENTRY HOLE

Entry holes of the proper size admit bluebirds while keeping starlings out. The hole recommended by the North American Bluebird Society is round and 1 1/2 inches in diameter. It has worked well all over the nation.

Years of study led Dick Peterson to question the choice of a round hole, since bluebirds are not round. The 1 1/2-inch round hole is wider than it needs to be, yet so restrictive in height that bluebirds have to crouch to get past it. Adult bluebirds can't tend the nestlings through the standard 1 1/2-inch hole without actually entering and leaving the box.

Peterson's houses now are built with an oblong entry hole, 1 3/8 inches wide and 2 1/4 inches high. This hole allows bluebirds to cling outside the box and feed the young or remove fecal sacs without entering the nest. Yet field experience shows the oblong hole stops starlings as

1019

*Opposite: Bluebird nests are built mainly with dry grasses.*

*– Bill Marchel Photo*

***A great source of wood for houses is construction sites. The amount of lumber they just throw away is incredible. Usually what you find is Douglas fir, a good wood for boxes. You can even find cedar scraps in some lumber yards.***

*– Dave Ahlgren*

well as the round hole.

A Texas study suggests starlings there get past entry holes that stop starlings in the upper Midwest. It might be necessary to go to a narrower hole in some regions. Peterson's research has shown that bluebirds could use holes as narrow as 1 3/16 inches wide, although they had to move through sideways.

Holes often become enlarged after a lot of use. Squirrels or birds chip at the edges until the hole becomes large enough to admit starlings. Check your holes to make sure they are as tight as they should be.

## RECOMMENDED BOX DESIGNS

The boxes described below are not the "only" good ones, but include several proven designs. Sources for plans, kits or constructed boxes are listed in the Appendix. Check your library for books that deal with bluebirds or ways you can help birds. Many such books have plans for approved boxes.

### The NABS Box

Over the decades, more bluebirds have been raised out of the box recommended by the North American Bluebird Society than any other. Most approved nest box designs are variants of this NABS box developed by Lawrence Zeleny.

The NABS box is compact, light and easy to build. Though it is built in different sizes, the 4-inch by 4-inch interior dimension is used most often. The NABS box is easy to carry when you are toting a number of boxes to mount them. The simple saw cuts involved in its construction present few challenges to "all-thumbs" carpenters.

The basic NABS box opens from the top. Advocates of top-opening boxes feel that nesting bluebirds are less disturbed than in boxes that open from the front or side. Top-opening boxes have some disadvantages. Because you have to inspect them from above, you either carry a stepladder or you mount them low to the ground where cats and 'coons are a hazard. It is difficult to spot blowfly larvae with top-opening boxes because the parasites hide under the nest. If you can determine that blowflies are present,

the only way to eliminate them is by taking out the nest.

A variation of the NABS box opens from the side. In this box, one side of the box pivots on nails placed high so the panel swings up and out at the bottom for easier monitoring.

The NABS box lacks a simple way to trap sparrows in the box. People who use the NABS box or its variants usually use a box-type ground trap placed near the nest box, not in it.

### The Huber Flip-Flop Box

Joe Huber, of Heath, Ohio, has modified the NABS box in several ways. Huber's box is unique because it alone opens both from the top and the front. Brackets at the base of the front panel allow it to flip forward and down. Huber's box offers some advantages over the original NABS design. Because the front flips down for easy eye-level monitoring, Huber's box can be mounted high enough to discourage ground-based predators. Huber's box is easy to check for blowflies or ants. Since the flopping front panel is not permanently nailed to the rest of the box, it is easy to replace in case the old hole has been enlarged.

Even better, the flip-flopping front can be converted to a sparrow trap. Huber makes an alternate box front with a built-in sparrow trap. When a sparrow enters the house, it trips a wire that drops a plywood panel over the hole, preventing escape. Huber often builds his boxes with the sparrow trap as a permanent part of the front panel.

The Appendix lists the address for details of Huber's box and his sparrow trap panel.

### The Peterson Box

In the eyes of many bluebirders, Dick Peterson has developed the most sophisticated and effective nest box. Because the front panel is interchangeable, this box sometimes is called a "system." This unique, angular box is highly attractive to bluebirds and exceptionally convenient for trail monitors.

The odd shape of the Peterson box has several advantages. Cats and raccoons can't perch conveniently on the steeply angled top to swipe in the hole. Similarly, the angled front panel offers predators a less secure perch,

*Opposite: Bluebirds spend a great deal of time perched near the ground.*

*– Steve Maslowski Photo*

***Ground traps, or flat box-like traps are super for catching the young-of-the-year sparrows. They aren't as good for smart, adult sparrows. The only way I know to catch the most dangerous adult sparrows is with an in-house trap.***

"CAUTION: THIS TRAP REQUIRES
SPECIAL ATTENTION. NEGLIGENT

and young bluebirds more easily climb out this sloping front at fledging time. The extended roof protects the hole against sun and rain.

The oblong hole makes the interior of the box more accessible to bluebirds, allowing them to feed the young and remove fecal sacs more conveniently. But the oblong hole is not a necessary feature of the Peterson box. Anyone who distrusts the oblong hole can build this box with a round hole or a tighter oblong hole instead.

Since the Peterson box is tapered toward the bottom, bluebirds can fill it quickly with nesting material. The small base offers less habitat for blowflies. The front-opening box makes it easy to check for blowflies or other insects and get rid of them. The floor can be pre-drilled to accept cotton swabs dipped in ant poison in case of ant infestation. Opening the box in the fall makes it unattractive to mice or squirrels in winter.

You can easily replace the front with a trap-front when sparrows are using a box. Peterson has developed an effective plexiglass sparrow trap, similar to the Huber trap. One trap front will serve about 20 to 30 houses. When you eliminate the sparrows using one box, move the trap front to another box, and so forth. The Peterson box is slightly heavier than most. The angled shape requires more complex angled cuts than the NABS box, making it more difficult for amateur craftsmen to build. The oblong entry hole is made best with a drill press. Still, constructing a Peterson box is not a forbiddingly difficult task.

If you doubt your carpentry skills, the most convenient way to build Peterson boxes is from kits. The Appendix

*Opposite: This trap front can be slipped into a Peterson box to trap sparrows. The trap is cocked.*

*– Steve Grooms Photo*

***People sometimes say it is silly to worry about the "convenience" of the adults as they feed the young. But remember, those birds must make about 240 to 320 trips a day to feed nestlings. If each trip involves a good deal more stooping or wasted motion running in and out of the box, that can be significant.***

***In the early decades of this century, people put up simple "birdhouses" that duplicated natural cavities. Many had roomy entry holes. Since the spread of starlings, those boxes have become dangerous. Avoid "birdhouses." Use nest boxes specifically designed for bluebirds, with tight holes, ventilation and provisions for monitoring.***

*Opposite: The trap has been triggered so a window now covers the only escape route.*

*– Steve Grooms Photo*

***I had a trail along a marsh where raccoons were wiping me out year after year until I went to the Noel guard. I have had 100 percent success since then!***

*– Richard Hjort*

lists sources of plans for Peterson boxes and inexpensive pre-cut kits.

### Other Designs

There are many other designs, each with its champions. A box with a slot opening (an opening extending from one side of the box to the other) might allow bluebirds to escape when assaulted by sparrows. Evidence suggests that sparrows avoid boxes with shallow bottoms. Some experimental PVC plastic boxes with shallow bottoms seem to keep sparrow problems to a minimum without sacrifices in other areas.

The perfect box has yet to be invented. Such a box would be convenient for monitors, attractive to bluebirds, weatherproof and perfectly repellent to predators. Of those criteria, the trickiest challenge is presented by predators. We now can engineer boxes that are safe against every predator *except* the house sparrow.

## CLIMBING PREDATOR GUARDS

The most popular predator guard is a panel around the entry hole that increases the hole's depth. This "predator block" is a piece of wood 3/4-inches to as much as 1 1/2 inches thick. The theory behind this guard is that a cat or raccoon will not be able to reach through this double thickness and still be able to grab bluebirds inside.

Reports about the effectiveness of this guard vary widely. Some users consider it perfect while others call it "useless." Those differences might reflect different levels of raccoon populations. Sometimes this guard works until a

***On one trail, you might not have raccoon problems for years, then something happens. Suddenly the raccoons in your area are motivated to look for every possible source of food. Boxes that have been secure for years might get hit one after the other. Your raccoon problems can change enormously from year to year.***

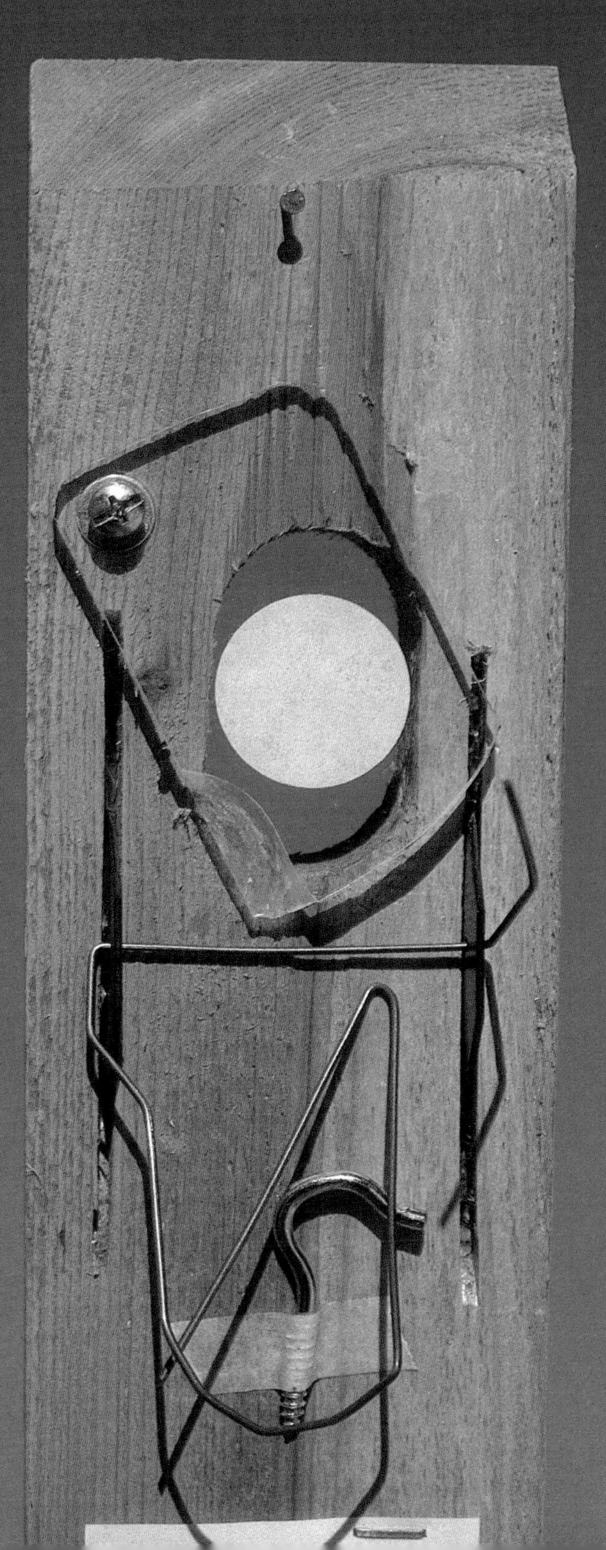

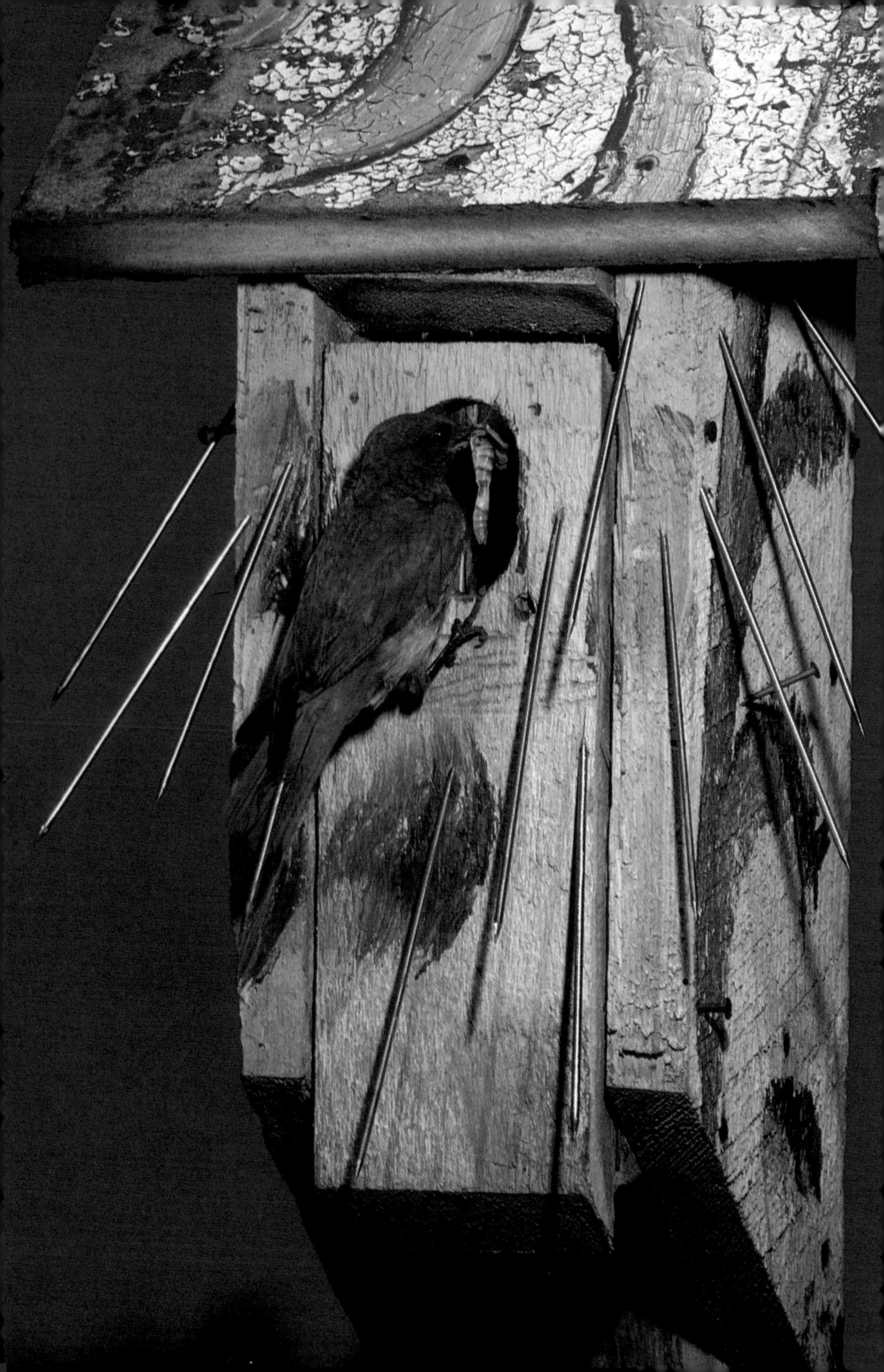

year of food shortage makes raccoons more desperate. It works best on deep boxes where the monitor artificially lowers the nest, keeping it several inches below the hole.

Bluebirds avoid thickened holes if thinner ones are available because thick holes require the birds to completely enter the box for routine chores. Dr. Zeleny has determined that entry holes with a total thickness over 1 1/2 inches are avoided by bluebirds if they have access to shallower holes.

Dick Peterson did well for years with a cat-coon guard involving a pair of 1/4-inch wooden dowels mounted on the front of the box. The pegs interfered with the ability of a predator to maneuver its paw to snatch the occupants. He no longer recommends it because something much better has come along.

No guard yet devised works as well as the one recently invented by Jim Noel of Ashland, Illinois. Noel's guard is built of the wire mesh called "hardware cloth." The material is fashioned into a square that mounts around the hole. Predators cannot reach inside the box and are discouraged from trying by sharp wires on the edge of the guard that hit them in the armpit. After a period of time, bluebirds adjust to this guard. On trails where raccoons routinely beat every other guard, the Noel guard completely stopped predation. It is usually put in place after nest-building has begun. Use a heavy grade of cloth. For maximum protection, sharpen the points of the wires with a file. A source for Noel Wire Coon Guards is in the Appendix.

There is no sparrow guard, as sparrows can go anywhere a bluebird can. People long have sought ways to discourage sparrows from using bluebird houses. One sparrow-spooker is at least somewhat effective. This involves a dowel mounted like a flagpole on the box. Four thin ribbons of mylar trail down from the top, just long enough to brush the box top. The fluttering mylar keeps some sparrows away from bluebird boxes. But *nothing* eliminates the need to trap sparrows.

Your most serious predator might be human. Boxes sited in areas of high human traffic might need some locking device on the door, such as a Phillips screw instead of the usual nail.

*Opposite: This type of predator guard has never been beaten, but might cause injuries to humans that would lead to lawsuits.*

– Dick Peterson Photo

***An adult coon weighing 18 pounds has a 20 inch reach. He can use that reach to beat the standard predator block.***

## FIGURE 6

## THE PETERSON NEST BOX (THREE-QUARTER VIEW)

This illustration, based on a drawing and design by Dick Peterson, gives an exploded view of the most popular and successful bluebird nesting box. Experimentation with variations on this design, according to local conditions and needs, is encouraged.

### MATERIAL LIST SUGGESTIONS

| Component | Suggested Material |
|---|---|
| Box Back<br>Inside Top<br>Inside Bottom | Standard 2x4 boards; actual dimensions: 1 1/2" x 3 1/2" |
| Swing-open Front | 3/4" solid wood (best choices cedar or Douglas fir), cut to 3 7/16" wide. Rough up below hole for foot hold – DO NOT USE PERCH! |
| Box Top & Sides | 3/4" exterior plywood or siding |
| Nails: | 7-penny coated box; 1" galvanized for swing-open front |
| Paint | Light tones – brown, green, gray (or leave natural) |

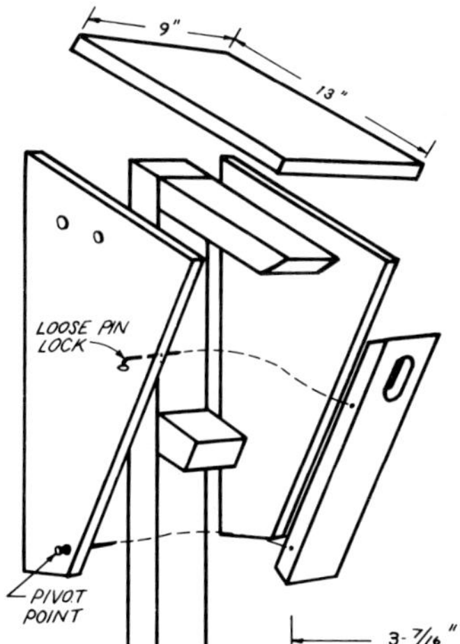

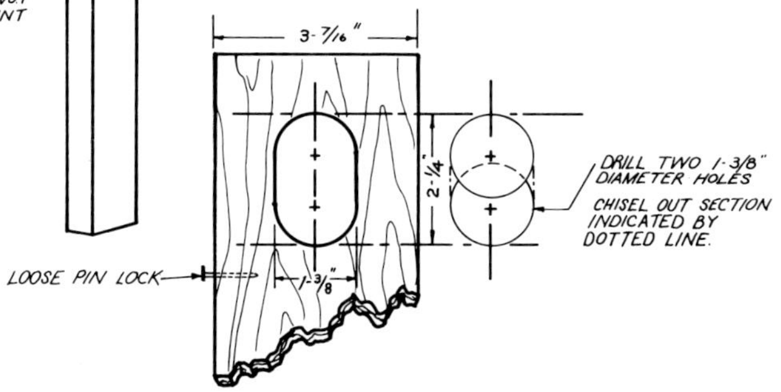

*Opposite: Though the male often hauls nest materials to the cavity site, the female actually constructs the nest.*

*– Bill Marchel Photo*

***In all my years of trailing, I've had exactly three starlings get in the boxes. Only one pair nested. Research shows me I can reduce the hole size so the skinniest starling can't enter it. But what would be the point? The hole I use keeps starlings out and is much more convenient for bluebirds.***

*Opposite: Bluebirds eat a great many insects considered undesirable by humans.*

*– Robert W. Baldwin Photo*

***Woods like redwood that used to be weather-resistant no longer are. The wood sold in lumber stores is now second-growth timber. Because it grew faster, it has wide growth rings and poor weather resistance. But the cedar you buy today is first-growth, with tight rings and good weathering properties.***

*– Dave Ahlgren*

## FIGURE 7

## PETERSON NEST BOX (Side View)

This detail of the Peterson nest box, with "ghosted" views of interior components, shows the relationship of all the parts and how they fit together.

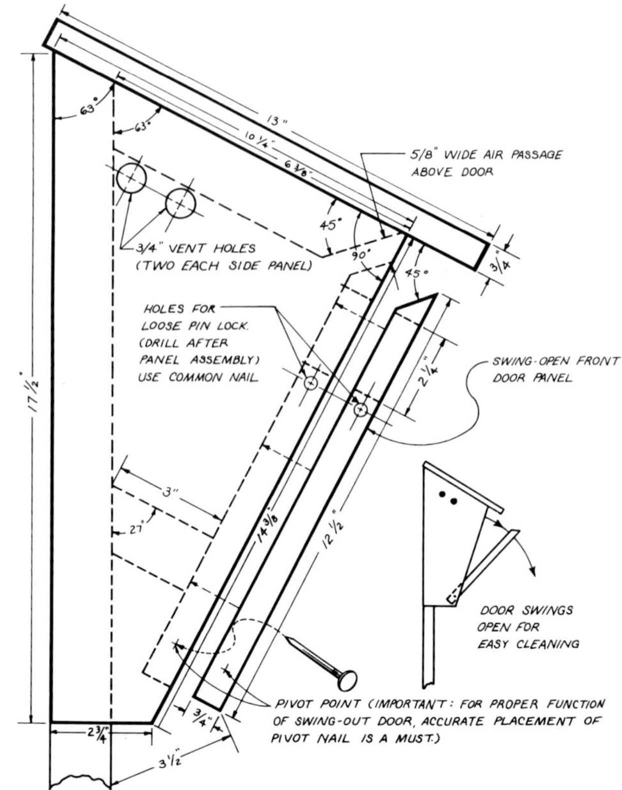

*Opposite: A goldfinch on a bluebird nest box. Bluebirds are territorial with respect to other bluebirds, but not against other species.*

*– Robert W. Baldwin Photo*

## FIGURE 8

## THE ORIGINAL NABS BOX

This nesting box design allows for a to-opening access. Use 1 3/4" galvanized siding nails or aluminum nails to fasten boards, 1 1/4" nails for dowel. Drill 3/32" holes in dowel for easy nailing. With top in place, hold cleat in exact position for nailing by reaching through bottom of box before bottom board is attached. Cut 3/8" off each corner (diagonally) of bottom board, as shown.

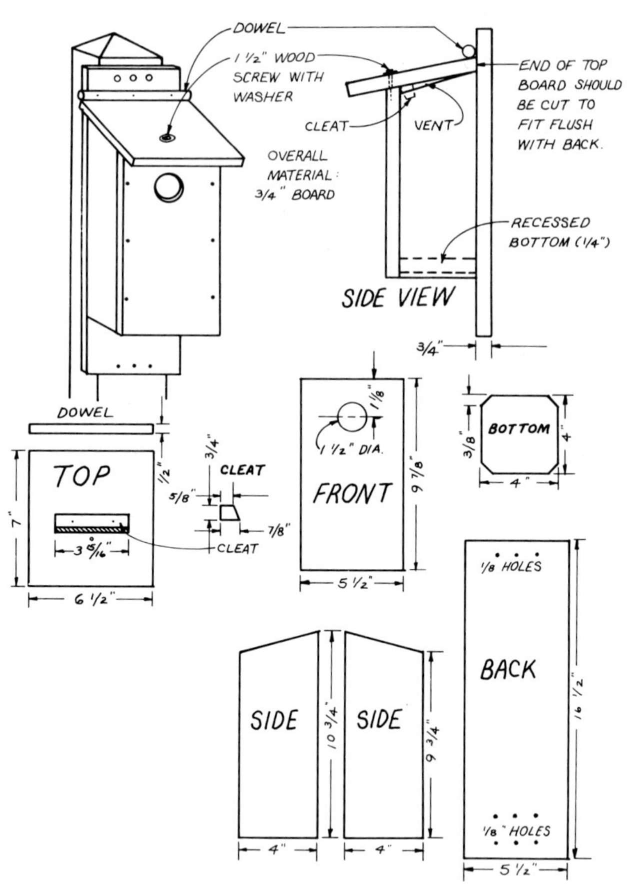

## FIGURE 9

## THE NEWER ZELENY NABS BOX

This is a side-opening variation of the original NABS box. Dimensions shown are for 3/4"- thick boards. Use 1 3/4" galvanized siding nails or aluminum nails. Pivot nails must be located exactly opposite each other as shown for proper opening of the side board. Cut 3/8" off each corner (diagonally) of bottom board, as shown. Top edges of front and back boards must be cut at a slight angle to fit flush with top board. Bottom board should be inserted so that woodgrain runs front to rear of box.

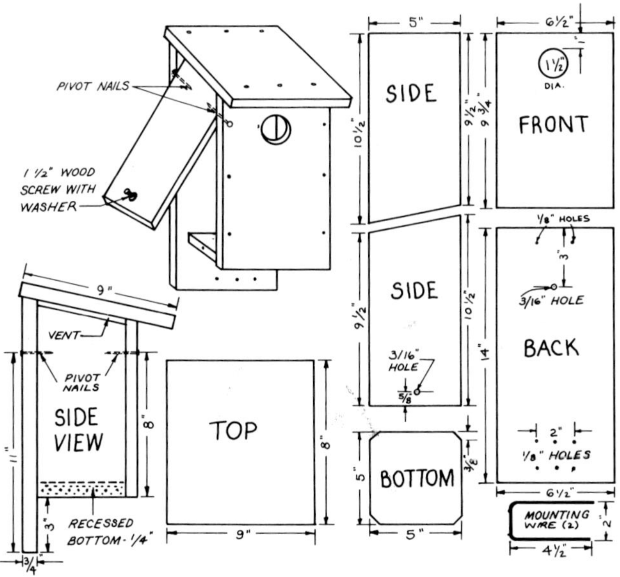


*Opposite: Peg predator guards make it difficult for cats to get at box occupants, though better guards now exist.*

*– Dick Peterson Photo*

*Following Spread: Wrens, a desirable and protected bird, can nonetheless wreak havoc on a bluebird trail.*

*– Dick Peterson Photo*

# Setting Up Your Bluebird Trail

Bluebirds won't use your boxes unless you set them out in proper bluebird habitat. One of the skills of running a trail is knowing when a box should be moved to a more promising location.

Bluebirds feed where they find perches near sunny openings. Perches are rarely a problem, as many natural or manmade objects suffice. Sunny openings are found around pastures, abandoned orchards, cemeteries, parks, walking or bicycling paths, gardens, rural meadows, gravel pits, clearings around farms, woodland openings, along many country roads and on golf courses.

Never erect boxes in areas sprayed with insecticides. Avoid golf courses that are sprayed indiscriminately; courses sprayed only on the greens are safe. Golf courses treated with herbicides but not pesticides are probably safe. Virtually all active orchards are heavily sprayed, as are some roadsides. Consider talking to the groundskeepers of golf courses or cemeteries to see if they might discontinue or reduce pesticide use. Amazingly, a great deal of spraying is done without much reason or thought.

Boxes mounted near woody, brushy areas are likely to attract house wrens. Wrens compete with bluebirds for houses, even to the point of destroying bluebird eggs or ejecting tiny bluebird nestlings. Place bluebird houses at least 100 feet away from dense shrubs or trees where wrens are likely to live. Wrens can be almost as dangerous and persistent as sparrows, and you can't eliminate the protected wren.

Human beings might be the peskiest nuisance animal on your trail. People occasionally destroy or steal bluebird boxes for no reason. More innocently, some people will open a box just before the young are ready to fledge. On public lands, such as parks, put boxes in the most remote corners where people rarely go.

Unless people are tampering with your boxes, there is no cause to site houses away from humans. Bluebirds are happy to be near people. They use boxes placed alongside apartment complexes, homes, roads or even railroads.

*Opposite: A bluebird perched in a cedar.*

*– Steve Maslowski Photo*

***Of all perches, nothing attracts bluebirds like dead branches. They really go for them.***

***An 18-hole golf course might have enough good habitat to support up to 75 bluebird houses.***

*– Lawrence Zeleny*

## SETTING UP YOUR BLUEBIRD TRAIL

Bluebirds nest in houses attached to rural mailboxes. If you can find a place near people where bluebirds will be treated with respect and where the house sparrow is not prevalent, bluebirds will nest there.

Because the house sparrow, the archenemy of the bluebird, is mostly an urban bird, bluebirds have been pushed to the outer fringes of suburbs and to rural areas. That means rural bluebird trails are much more likely to be successful than urban trails.

Yet it is possible to raise bluebirds in urban areas. If you choose to try, keep several things in mind. You might need to wait a long time, perhaps several years, before your first bluebirds appear. There simply aren't many bluebirds flying around modern cities in spring looking for nesting cavities. Anyone hoping to raise bluebirds in urban areas must become an industrious-even ruthless-sparrow trapper. Sparrows are not a protected species. Quite the contrary, sparrows and starlings should be controlled with continuous trapping. Bluebirds and sparrows absolutely will not coexist. People have often tried to raise bluebirds without bothering sparrows. It doesn't work! Go to work on sparrows *before* you discover your first clutch of baby bluebirds with pierced skulls.

Trapping sparrows out of an urban area might seem like empyting the ocean with a spoon. You'll obviously never get them all. Yet sparrows don't move around to replace unoccupied habitat as rapidly as some birds do, so trapping can suppress their numbers in local areas. You can create a sparrow-free zone where bluebirds can safely live and nest.

When siting a bluebird trail, keep in mind the practical realities of monitoring. The ideal trail is set out in a long circular route so you can hike the loop from box to box, ending up where you started. That ideal is difficult to realize. Some bluebirders put out boxes along country roads so they can monitor them with automobiles. If you have a long, straight trail, it helps to have a friend who can drop you off and drive ahead to pick you up. Or consider monitoring with a mountain bike.

Avoid the temptation to set boxes out along fencelines. It is the most natural and convenient arrangement . . . for you and any predators that decide to monitor your trail. Fencelines make natural "predator highways."

*Opposite: Nest boxes with entry holes barely the size of a bluebird keep out many predators.*

*– Bill Marchel Photo*

***Three unproductive years – three years when bluebirds don't use a box – are a good clue that you should move that box to a better location.***

*Opposite: Bluebirds among apple blossoms, a wonderful habitat that has largely been lost of bluebirds because of insecticide spraying.*

*– Steve Maslowski Photo*

***One of our greatest joys is getting other people involved in bluebirds. We go to their place and help them set up their boxes and we even tell them where the bluebirds will perch. It isn't that hard when you know bluebirds. Then they call us up, all excited, and say they've got bluebirds sitting right where we told them they would!***

*– Richard Hjort*

Since few of us own land with ideal bluebird habitat, we usually place our boxes on someone else's land. *Always* get permission first! That is usually easy. People love bluebirds. When you explain why bluebirds need help, most private landowners and public agencies are delighted to cooperate. It helps if your houses are attractive. Once bluebirds begin using the houses, invite the landowners to come along to see them. They will be thrilled and proud to see the beautiful birds being produced on their land.

You may have to decide between establishing a trail on your own property or one in a more distant area with better bluebird habitat. The closer your trail is to where you live, the easier it will be to monitor. If you raise bluebirds near your home, you can feed them and enjoy their presence every day.

Yet often the wiser course is to set up a more remote trail in habitat where bluebirds are more likely to succeed. This kind of question is best answered by experienced bluebirders in your own area.

## MOUNTING BOXES

Boxes should be mounted as high as possible while being accessible for monitoring. Side- or front-opening boxes should be mounted so the base of the box is close to eye-level. That means the base of the box will be five or six feet above ground. Top-opening boxes must be set about four feet above ground unless you will carry a ladder to check them. In areas with high human traffic, it sometimes is necessary to mount boxes ten feet high to keep people from meddling with them.

Mount boxes so the hole points away from the hot afternoon sun and the prevailing winds. Boxes should face north, east or northeast whenever possible. Along unpaved roads, mount boxes with the hole facing away from the dust kicked up by cars.

Ideally, a bluebird box should be mounted near some convenient perch, with a shrub or fence or some low object within 60 feet to receive the young on their first flight. If you mount boxes near pastures, you have to place them where cattle can't relieve itchy skins by rubbing against them.

The best mount of all is a galvanized steel pipe, one-

*Above: Grasshoppers are among the most important insects to bluebirds.*

*– Steve Maslowski Photo*

*Opposite: Tree swallows make nests with large, white feathers.*

*– Dick Peterson Photo*

*Opposite: Bluebirds nest in cavities in wooden fence poles something like this one.*

*– Steve Maslowski Photo*

***Many states have a program encouraging community groups to "Adopt a Highway." Citizen groups accept responsibility for removing litter from certain stretches of roadsides. A natural and desirable extension of that program would be for groups to put bluebird houses on their adopted stretches of highway.***

***I had a lot of trouble with predators until last year when I wrapped my poles with sheet metal. I used sheets of metal from a printing shop. That totally stopped the predation.***

*– Rita Efta*

inch in diameter or less. Nothing gives climbing predators less to grasp than a smooth steel pipe. The common metal T-shaped fencepost works well, though these have knobby surfaces that give raccoons a climbing grip. Better, though harder to find, is the taller metal post built to carry highway signs.

Posts of slippery PVC plastic have worked very well for some people. Use 1 1/2- or 2-inch PVC pipe. Another new post that seems highly predator-proof is a "rebar" (concrete reinforcement bar) slipped inside a piece of 3/4-inch conduit.

Avoid wood poles whenever possible, as they are easily climbed and hard to make predator-proof. If you must mount a box on a wood fencepost, elevate the box and put a climbing guard under it. Telephone companies object to finding boxes mounted on their utility poles; if you ask their permission, they may give it. Mounting a box directly on a tree is just inviting predation.

## CLIMBING GUARDS

The three climbing predators of concern are raccoons, cats and snakes. You can defeat them several ways.

A very effective climbing guard is a cone of metal shaped like a "coolie hat." This should be no less than 24 inches in diameter. Placed around a pole, this guard can't be bypassed by climbing predators even if the pole is wood. It works quite well and is the only guard that can stop a snake. Place houses with these guards with care. These guards often get squashed or knocked loose by livestock or farmers' tractors. Horses and cattle like to scratch their noses on the edges of these guards.

Sheets of aluminum wrapped around wood posts form a slippery surface predators can't shinny past. Newspapers can supply used "printer's tins" at very little cost for this purpose. Apply these guards carefully so there are no ridges or surfaces predators can get a claw into. Mount them up near the box, at least four feet above the ground, and use enough metal to create a 20-inch expanse of slippery metal.

Some trailers coat posts with a liberal layer of automobile axle grease or a product called Tanglefoot. Grease or Tanglefoot won't always work on wood poles, and you have to keep checking them to make sure the

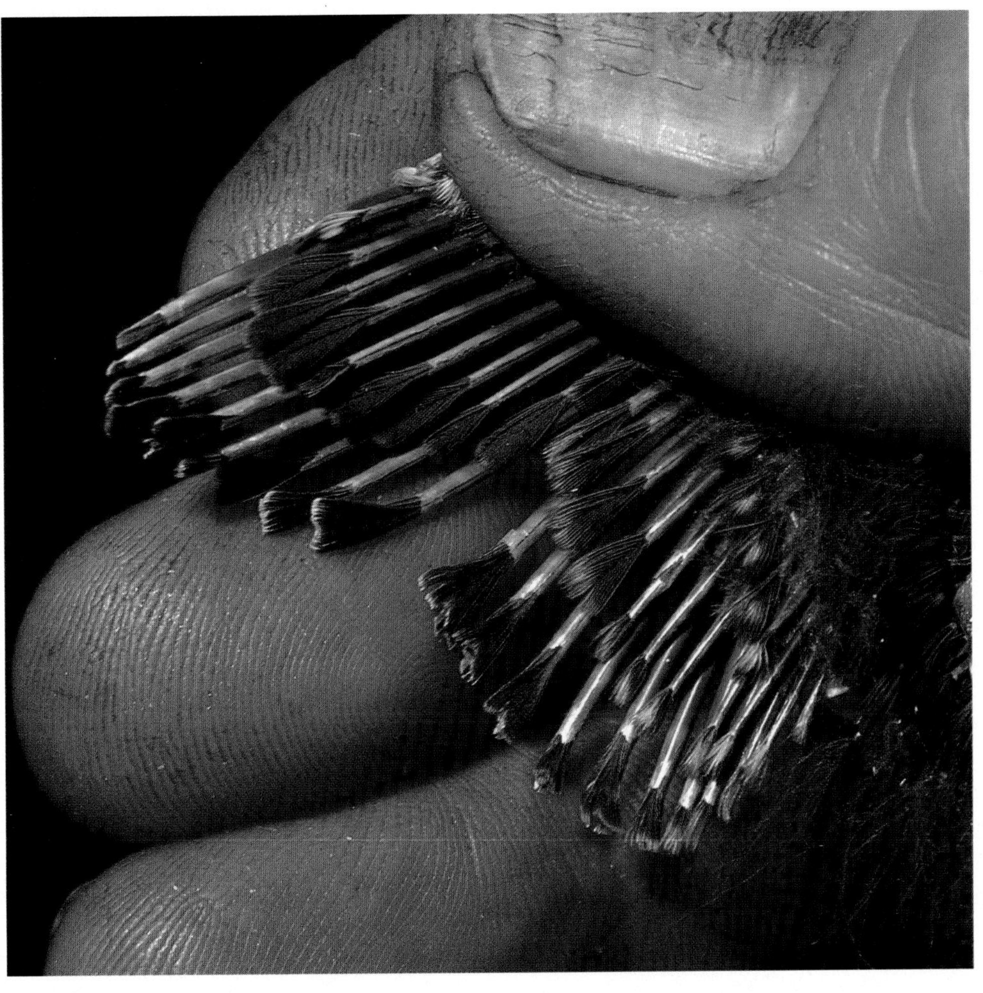

*Opposite: Bluebirds are hard-working, devoted parents.*

*– Dick Peterson Photo*

*Above: The wing of a nestling twelve days old. Note that the primary feathers have now erupted from the quill.*

*– Dick Peterson Photo*

*Opposite: Compared to the nests of many birds, bluebird nests are neat and homogenous.*

*– Bill Marchel Photo*

*Above: Berries are particularly important to bluebirds in winter. Starlings now hog much of this food.*

*– Steve Maslowski Photo*

grease hasn't been sun-baked or absorbed by the wood. These products will stop ants and-sometimes-snakes. Because they are petroleum-based, these greases are avoided when possible by ecologically concerned bluebirders. And there have been problems with small birds dying after getting stuck in Tanglefoot.

*Opposite: A female bluebird in a privet.*

*– Steve Maslowski Photo*

## SPACING AND PAIRING

Consider the territorial requirements of bluebirds when spacing boxes along your trail. Bluebirds need a certain distance between their nests to assure they will find enough food to sustain their young. If your bluebird houses are closer than 100 yards apart, the birds will have territorial conflicts and some boxes won't be used. Closer spacing is possible in situations where you are feeding bluebirds or where the birds at one house do not have a direct line of sight to another nearby house.

***I'm all in favor of pairing boxes. There are just so many benefits. I once saw a pair of tree swallows drive a kestrel away that was near a pair of boxes. They just dove at him and harassed him until he had to leave. Tree swallows can offer protection to bluebirds in the paired box.***

Bluebirds do accept birds of other species near their nests, which led to the practice of *pairing* boxes. This involves placing two boxes about 20 feet apart, each pair of boxes separated from other pairs by 100 yards. Pairing offers many advantages. Quite often a tree swallow will nest in one box, with a bluebird in the paired box. Swallows are desirable birds and harmless to bluebirds. Like bluebirds, they are under pressure from starling infestations. Swallows sometimes defend both boxes against wrens and sparrows, two species that threaten bluebirds.

Pairing reduces the amount of direct competition for boxes. Wrens, swallows or sparrows often drive the bluebirds from a nest box. But if there is another box right at hand, the intruders go to it instead. That gives you the chance to deal with them.

*Opposite: Seven-day old nestlings, as seen by their parents.*

*– Dick Peterson Photo*

*Above: Dave Ahlgren shows a youngster how to build a bluebird nest box.*

*– Steve Grooms Photo*

# Problems and Solutions Along the Trail

Would you like to come along to help me monitor a bluebird trail? Actually, we're going to cheat a little. Through the magic of Poetic License, we'll compress events that might happen over six months of trailing into one trip around the boxes.

Our trail happens to be a fairly long one that we can walk. We'll load a knapsack with cold drinks and candy bars. Don't forget the binoculars, the sparrow trap apparatus, insect repellant, a Swiss Army knife and some pyrethrin spray. And of course, a notebook and pen.

Before heading out, we'll spray our boots and pants legs with a repellant containing pyrethrin as a precaution against ticks that might carry Lyme disease. And we'll pack along some thin rubber gloves in case we have to handle mice, as they host the ticks that carry the disease.

We'll visit the first box in early March. We haven't looked at it since September. We want to make sure the box is clean and in good shape before the first bluebirds appear. Since this box lacks an opening front, we weren't able to open it for the winter. Whoops! We have a nest of white-footed mice here. Put the gloves on. Scram, guys! Check the condition of the box. If it has drain holes, make sure they are clear. Is the entry hole nice and tight? Any major cracks in the wood? Okay, this one's bluebird-ready.

The next box we come to is in late April. As we approach it, we make soft noises to tell any bluebirds here that we are coming. We don't want to startle them. Tap gently on the box before opening it. Wow, there goes the female! Great, bluebirds are nesting here!

If we check this box frequently, always giving the bluebirds reassuring advance notice, the female soon will pay no attention when we open her box. In fact, she might barely notice us. To help bluebirds accept you without fussing, come around often enough and never act like a predator. Always give the female an escape route when opening the box. Let's inspect the contents of this box. It seems she has nearly completed the nest. We'll want to get back to this box pretty soon so we can note the time she

*Opposite: Natural cavities are not plentiful enough now to sustain bluebird numbers.*

*– Steve Maslowski Photo*

***A humane way to take mice or birds out of your box, especially if it is a top-opening box, is to spray Prestone brand starter fluid in the box. It contains ether, which puts them to sleep.***

*Above: Bluebirds on a nest box display courtship rapture in the middle of a major urban area.*

*– Dick Peterson Photo*

*Opposite: Hungry little mouths wait for a protein-rich grasshopper.*

*– Dick Peterson Photo*

*Opposite: Enjoying a private moment, this pair displays the family closeness characteristic of all bluebirds.*

*– Ted Thousand Photo*

***If bluebirds think you are a threat to their nest, they might dive-bomb you. Don't worry. They won't hurt you. And don't worry that they will abandon their nest or babies if you fiddle with them. That's a myth.***

***A little trick will tell you whether the female is incubating the eggs or not. Put an egg to your lips. If it is cold, she's not done laying eggs. If it is warm, she's incubating already.***

first lays eggs. Jot that down in the notebook.

Our next box had a bluebird nest in it the last time we checked. Today, though, things look strange. There seems to be another nest over the bluebird nest. The top nest is coarser and incorporates a number of large white feathers. That tells us a tree swallow is nesting here. A desirable and protected bird, the tree swallow is under pressure from starlings just as the bluebird is. By law, we can't disturb this nest. Instead, we'll put up another bluebird box 25 feet away, hoping the bluebirds will move there to nest again. We probably should have paired all boxes along this trail in the first place.

The next box we come to is maybe a little close to some woods. Actually, what happened was that the brush has grown since we mounted it. Sure enough, this box is filled with little sticks, the handiwork of a male wren. But we are in luck because there is no wren nest yet built among the sticks. But we better act quickly.

We can do three things. We can clean out the wren's hodgepodge of sticks, hoping that will discourage him. We can move this box out farther from the brush where a bluebird might use it. If it is far enough from cover, the wrens might stay away. Better yet, let's move this box closer to the brush and put another one out more in the open where a bluebird can nest in safety. Wrens are nice birds and protected by law, though they sure can be pesky on a bluebird trail. Nobody has yet invented a guard that will keep a wren out of a bluebird house.

Things are quiet at the next box. No sign of life at all. You know, this box has been here four years without seeing use. Maybe the grass is too high for bluebirds to spot insects here. Time to move it to a new spot.

Our next box has four bluebird eggs. The female will probably lay another egg and then begin incubating. Make a note. We'll want to know later just when this box's eggs are due to hatch.

The next box presents sad news. The debris of bluebird eggs lies around the box. Inside we find a messy nest full of paper, weeds and other debris laid on top of the bluebird nest. This is the nasty work of house sparrows. If we'd monitored more often, we might have prevented this attack by getting rid of the sparrows weeks ago.

Fortunately, the adults are still living.

Though we are late, we can act. This box has a front opening door. We can drop the front and slip in a sparrow trap front. We can set the trap now and run the rest of the trail, then come back to see if we've caught our sparrows.

We're going to use an advanced trick here. We've been carrying an extra house in our knapsack just for this purpose. It looks just like our other boxes, but is made of thin plywood to keep its weight to a minimum. And it has a permanent trap front. We'll hang it right on the box mounted permanently here.

Sparrows are extremely persistent and resourceful. If we throw out their nests, they'll build again. And again and again. When a male sparrow forms a bond with a cavity, he never relinquishes it. Even if we trap and remove several females from "his" box, the male will continue to claim it, bringing in more and more females. So we have to get him.

Our best plan is to trap him. Flat box-type sparrow traps placed near the box often do the job. They are very effective against juvenile sparrows, less effective on the smarter, older sparrows. Of several models available, the Cedar Valley Trap (see Appendix) is probably the best. These box traps offer the best way to work down populations of sparrows in a local area.

Yet nothing matches an in-house trap for eliminating the sparrows plaguing a particular box. The Peterson and Huber sparrow traps are triggered by a wire lever the sparrow hits as it enters the box. The trigger drops a panel over the entry hole, trapping the sparrow (the male, we hope) inside. Since these devices also trap bluebirds or swallows, they *must not* be left untended for any length of time. When you set them, you have to return to them within hours.

We come now to a box in early May. And, yes, it has baby bluebirds! We lower the box front to reveal four nestlings with imploring open mouths. Since the adults at this box know us by now, they do not appear the least bit concerned as we gently touch the babies.

But here's trouble. Below the babies in the nest material we find blowfly larvae.Disgusting things! Along with gnats and blackflies, blowflies are the most serious parasites of

*Opposite: Gentle and loving, bluebirds seem to want to do everything in pairs or family groups.*

*– Steve Maslowski Photo*

***Snakes have an amazing ability to get into birdhouses. They often confuse people because they leave no clues. If you find your eggs or nestlings just suddenly gone without anything else being disturbed, that is the clue that a snake has struck.***

bluebirds. Blowflies don't actually kill nestlings, though they can weaken them to the point they succumb to hypothermia or malnutrition. Blowflies often infest nests that get wet, so we'll want to make sure this box is watertight.

Fortunately, the front of this box opens so we can see under the nest. If we carefully lift the nest, babies and all, with our knife and tap the nesting material, we'll dislodge the larvae. We whisk them away, then lower the nest and close the box. If the infestation had been more serious – say, 50 larvae or more – we would have sprayed the lower nest with pyrethrin, a natural insecticide and the only one that is safe for birds. No need this time.

We approach our next box with care, as we know it has nestlings close to fledging. Remember, nestlings usually fledge at 17 or 18 days of age, and our records show that this gang is about 19 days old. Remember, too, the nestlings will never return to the box if spooked into bailing out prematurely.

We'll stop some distance from the box and use the glasses to watch. A parent will arrive every five minutes with food if nestlings are in the box. If the parents fail to show after several minutes, check the box. We'll hope to find an empty nest, meaning that the nestlings have fledged. Wonderful! That's five more bluebirds. Make notes. We'll clean out the old nest to make this box ready for a second nesting, hopefully just as successful.

Uh-oh! The next box has been raided. Blue feathers are strewn below the box, nest material hangs halfway out the hole and the bluebirds are gone. No, wait. The adults are over there on the fence, singing plaintively. The nestlings have been lost, but not the parents.

The culprit had to have been a raccoon or a cat. A snake wouldn't have torn up the nest. This box was placed far from the usual haunts of cats but closer to a marsh than it should have been. Raccoons probably did this damage. You often have the worst raccoon problems with boxes near water. We'll remount this box on a thin steel pole with grease and a climbing guard and install a Noel guard over the hole. That will do it!

If this box had been near a farm or human dwellings, we'd have suspected a cat got the young, though feral cats

*Opposite: Two orphaned nestlings being reared by hand.*

*– Dick Peterson Photo*

***We consider that we are trying to help all cavity-nesting songbirds. We have tree swallows and chickadees and wrens using our boxes. The bluebird is the frosting on the cake, of course. You're always delighted to get them. But you shouldn't feel bad about helping other birds as well.***

*– Richard Hjort*

roam widely. Many people feel it is cruel to confine pet cats. They haven't witnessed the cruelty cats practice on birds. Had the predator of this box been a cat, we would have improved the box installation by giving it a big climbing guard and a Noel guard. Then we would put out a humane live trap to catch the cat. Feral cats can be dispatched. Pets should be turned over to the appropriate agency. Most communities have cat leash laws.

We probably should move this box now because at least one local raccoon knows about it. Once a raccoon learns a box can provide an easy meal, he is likely to sniff around for more. Raccoon problems often run in streaks, becoming bad when one or more animals in the area learn to get in nest boxes. Raccoons can learn to be trail monitors, too, which is one reason we need to avoid obvious locations when placing boxes in 'coon country.

Okay, we've reached the end of the trail. Let's return now to the traps we left for the sparrows. Aha, both boxes are occupied! Here is what happened. The female went into the box with the nest and tripped that little trap door. Then the male got upset. He dominates her and wants her in sight at all times. Losing caution, he entered the trap box we set up. By using the second box, we can often trap the female and the male within a few minutes instead of several days.

We want to get these birds out without hurting them. After all, the birds might not be sparrows. In our pack is a soup can with no top or bottom. A rubber band holds a plastic baggie over one end. If we lift the trap door and hold this can to the entry hole, the sparrow will fly toward the light, right into the baggie.

Well, now it is time to go home. We've come a long way, having checked a great many boxes, walking through about four months along the way. The sun is just about to droop behind those trees to the southwest.

What's that? Look. The bluebirds at that corner box are still hauling food for their nestlings. As hard as we've walked today, they've put in a harder day. It is fun to think, as we walk toward the car, that we have been working toward the same end as that bluebird couple. Just as they do, we want to see that there are more bluebirds in this world.

*Opposite: Bluebirds sometimes hover over prey they are hunting.*

*– Steve Maslowski Photo*

***If you ever see the parents come with food but fail to deliver it, they are teasing the young so they will leave the nest. Stay back a bit. It's really cute to watch!***

*Top: Dick Peterson checking a Peterson box. Note the holes in the floor; they accept poison-dipped swabs in case of ant infestations.*

*– Dick Peterson Photo*

*Bottom: Mounting boxes on metal poles discourages predation, though raccoons can climb poles with knobby surfaces.*

*– Robert W. Baldwin Photo*

# Appendix

The best overall book on the eastern bluebird is probably still Dr. Lawrence Zeleny's **The Bluebird: How You Can Help It's Fight for Survival**. Zeleny addresses himself to a broad range of issues, including winter feeding and providing roosting boxes in wintering areas. The book discusses the two North American Bluebird Society (NABS) boxes, the top-opening and side-opening, presenting clear plans for making both. Diagrams illustrate box mounting techniques and predator guards. A $9.95 paperback from the Indiana Press, it is available from NABS, in which case there is a ten percent shipping and handling charge. Write: NABS, Box 6295, Silver Spring, MD 20906-0295.

The most comprehensive and useful "how-to" book for bluebird conservationists is Dorene H. Scriven's **Bluebirds in the Upper Midwest**. Scriven presents a broad range of insights and tips for helping bluebirds, often giving the reader the benefit of opposing points of view. The subtitle, "A Guide to Successful Trail Management," accurately reflects the emphasis. Scriven does, however, deal with such topics as sparrow trapping and raising mealworms. Though the book only claims to be about bluebird conservation in the upper Midwest, it is not limited by narrow regionalism. This $10.50 paperback is published by the Bluebird Restoration Program of the Audubon Chapter of Minneapolis. It is available from NABS or directly from the Bluebird Recovery Program, c/o Marlys Hjort, 9571 270th Street North, Chisago City, MN 55013.

For bluebirds with a southern accent, look at **Bluebirds** by Tina and Curtis Dew and R.B. (Reber) Layton. The first half of this book is comprised of correspondence from Tina Dew to Layton, detailing her adventures feeding bluebirds and helping them nest in Mississippi. The second half, by Layton, presents tips for helping bluebirds. The lively descriptions of daily contact with bluebirds is interesting, as is the southern slant. This book is available from NABS for $9.95 (for the soft cover edition) and $12.95 (for the hard cover edition), plus the ten percent shipping fee.

NABS is the national organization promoting bluebird conservation. A regular membership is only $15. The main benefit of membership is receiving *Sialia*, the quarterly national publication dealing with threats to the bluebird and the many different responses. NABS is also a very good source of books, tapes, merchandise (such as photographs of bluebirds, decals, bluebird sweatshirts, etc). A simple diagram showing construction details of a NABS is on the society's brochure. NABS sells completed nest boxes and kits. The address is: North American Bluebird Society, Box 6295, Silver Spring, MD 20906-0295.

The Bluebird Recovery Program of the Audubon Chapter of Minneapolis (BBRP) is an unusually active, hands-on group with extensive experience in bluebird conservation. The suggested annual donation for membership is only $5. Members receive full-size Peterson nest box blueprints, a brochure and

*Opposite: Though the thrush family is extremely widespread, only America has bluebirds.*

*– Steve Maslowski Photo*

quarterly newsletters that are lively and useful. Merchandise, books and video tapes are offered for sale. BBRP encourages members from other states to join or create their own local groups, but for $5 there is no reason to not also belong to this group, if just to listen in on the intense, on-going dialogue about new methods of helping bluebirds. Write to The Bluebird Recovery Program of the Audubon Chapter of Minneapolis, Box 3801, Minneapolis, MN 55403.

There is now no single source of information about how a person can contact the various local bluebird groups in this country and the several provinces of Canada. The best starting point is to contact your state or province's wildlife or natural resources agency. They will almost surely have an address or phone number for any group actively helping bluebirds in the area.

Joe Huber is happy to send plans for his Flip-Flop box and In-House Sparrow Trap. To cover his mailing costs, send a large self-addressed, stamped envelope and 50 cents to Joe Huber, 1720 Evergreen Court, Heath, OH 43056.

The best source of Peterson nest boxes and accessories is the Ahlgren Construction Company. Dave Ahlgren sells kits, assembled houses, sparrow trap fronts, Noel Cat/Coon guards and other birding products at his own cost. Prices in 1990 are about $7 for each Peterson box kit, plus $4 shipping for the first box kit, $2 shipping for each additional box kit. The Noel guard is $1.50, plus $2.25 shipping and handling for one-to-ten guards. The sparrow trap front sells for $5.50, plus $2.50 for shipping the first trap front, $1 for shipping each additional trap front. If you want a totally finished Peterson box, the cost is $9.50, plus $4 shipping and postage for the first box, $2 for shipping each additional box. Contact the Ahlgren Construction Company, 12989 Otchipwe Avenue North, Stillwater, MN 55082.